BUILDING PURPOSE
A GUIDE TO STARTING
YOUR NONPROFIT

Step one in starting your nonprofit is choosing a unique and meaningful name for your organization.

Flaca Alexis-Dalce

ISBN: 978-1-965666-75-3 (Paperback)
ISBN: 978-1-965666-76-0 (Hardcover)

Printed in the United States of America

Table of Contents

Step one in starting your nonprofit involves ensuring your organization's name is unique and aligns with your mission. Once your name is clear, follow these key steps:

1. Check State Requirements: Research your state's specific requirements for registering a nonprofit organization. These requirements vary by state, so be sure to comply with local regulations.

2. Register as a Nonprofit: Once you've chosen and confirmed the availability of your nonprofit name, register your business as a nonprofit organization with the appropriate state agency, usually the Secretary of State's office.

3. Report to the Financial Crimes Enforcement Network (FinCEN): Visit the FinCEN website to report to your nonprofit organization, ensuring transparency and compliance with financial regulations.

4. Apply for an EIN: Go to the IRS website to apply for an Employer Identification Number (EIN). This is essential for tax purposes and will allow you to open a bank account and hire employees.

5. Register with the IRS as a Nonprofit: Ensure you select the correct nonprofit designation (e.g., 501(c)(3)) when registering with the IRS for tax-exempt status.

6. Open a Bank Account: Choose a bank that offers services tailored for nonprofit organizations and open an account to manage your finances properly.

Charitable organization: Exemption application

To apply for exemption, a foundation should complete and submit Form 1023, Application for Recognition of Exemption under Section 501(c)(3) of the Internal Revenue Code, or Form 1023-EZ, Streamlined Application for Recognition of Exemption under Section 501(c)(3) of the Internal Revenue Code, on Pay.gov, along with the required user fee. If a foundation will be represented by an attorney or other representative, it must also submit a power of attorney. See When to File for a discussion of deadlines for filing an application.

Private operating foundations and certain other organizations cannot file a Form 1023-EZ. To learn more about this process and whether your organization is eligible refer to Revenue Procedure 2024-5 (updated annually).

Public disclosure requirements apply to exemption applications that the IRS approves. In addition, cases in which the IRS has issued a letter denying or revoking a foundation's exempt status are subject to public disclosure under Internal Revenue Code.

Organizations not required to file Form 1023

The following types of organizations are not required to file Form 1023 for recognition of exemption under Internal Revenue Code section 501(c)(3):

- Churches, including synagogues, temples and mosques.
- Integrated auxiliaries of churches and conventions or associations of churches.
- Any organization (other than a private foundation) that has gross receipts in each taxable year of normally not more than $5,000.

Contributors' contributions to these types of organizations are tax deductible. Although there is no requirement to do so, many churches and small organizations seek IRS recognition because recognition assures contributors that contributions are deductible.

Public charity - Tax exemption application

To be exempt under section 501(c)(3), an organization must file an application for recognition of exemption with the IRS. The law provides limited exceptions to the filing requirement.

File either Form 1023 or Form 1023-EZ to apply for exemption under section 501(c)(3). The applications have instructions, check sheets and worksheets to help you provide the information required to process your application. The IRS will not process an incomplete application.

See When to file for an explanation of the deadlines for filing an application.

Exceptions to application requirement

The following organizations are excepted from the exemption application requirement:

- Churches, their integrated auxiliaries, and conventions or associations of churches; and
- An organization that is not a private foundation and the gross receipts (total amounts the organization received from all sources during its annual accounting period, without subtracting any costs or expenses) of which in each taxable year are normally not more than $5,000.

Additional information

- Gross receipts test - Section 501(c)(3) exemption application
- Group exemptions - Publication 4573, Group Exemptions PDF

Interactive training

Learn more about the benefits, limitations and expectations of tax-exempt organizations by attending 10 courses at the online Small to mid-size tax exempt organization workshop.

1-STEP BY STEP FOR CHURCH APPLYING FOR 501C3

Applying for 501(c)(3) status for a church involves several steps. This process ensures that the church can be recognized as a tax-exempt nonprofit organization by the IRS. Below are the step-by-step instructions to apply for 501(c)(3) status:

1. Establish Your Church as a Legal Entity

Before applying for 501(c)(3) status, you need to establish your church as a legal entity. This usually involves the following steps:

- **Create a Name for Your Church**: Ensure the name is not already taken by checking your state's business registry.
- **Incorporate the Church**: File articles of incorporation with your state's business registration office (usually the Secretary of State). The articles should include the church's purpose and its mission, which must align with IRS regulations for tax-exempt purposes, like religious, educational, or charitable activities.
- **Draft Bylaws**: These are internal rules for governing the church. They outline the structure of your organization, leadership roles, and responsibilities, as well as other operational guidelines.

2. Obtain an Employer Identification Number (EIN)

Apply for an EIN from the IRS. This number acts like a Social Security Number for your church. You will need it to file the 501(c)(3) application and to open a bank account for the church.

- **Apply for EIN online**: You can get an EIN through the IRS website for free.

3. Ensure Your Church Qualifies

The IRS has specific requirements for religious organizations. Make sure your church qualifies for 501(c)(3) status by meeting the following conditions:

- **Organized for religious purposes**: The church must have a stated religious purpose in its articles of incorporation.
- **Operate for the public good**: The church must serve the public, not just its members.
- **No private inurement**: No part of the church's income should benefit private individuals (such as church founders, board members, or other insiders).
- **No political or lobbying activities**: The church should not be involved in political campaigning or excessive lobbying activities.

4. Prepare Form 1023 or Form 1023-EZ

The IRS provides two forms for applying for 501(c)(3) status:

- **Form 1023 (Long Form)**: This is the standard application for larger organizations or more complex cases. It requires detailed information about the church's history, finances, governance, and activities.
- **Form 1023-EZ (Short Form)**: This is a streamlined version for smaller churches that meet certain criteria. Your church can use this form if it has less than $50,000 in annual revenue and total assets under $250,000.

Instructions for Completing Form 1023/1023-EZ:

- **Part I: Basic Information**: Enter basic details such as the church's name, EIN, and contact information.
- **Part II: Structure**: Provide details on the church's structure, including whether it is a corporation, unincorporated association, or other legal entity.
- **Part III: Activities and Purpose**: Describe the church's religious activities, worship services, outreach programs, and other functions that support your mission.

- **Part IV: Financial Information**: Provide financial statements, including projected budgets for the next three years if the church is new. You may also need to include past financial records if the church has been operating.
- **Part V: Compensation**: Detail compensation provided to church leaders and staff to show that they are reasonable and not benefiting insiders unfairly.
- **Part VI: Public Charity Status**: Confirm that the church qualifies as a public charity, which means it will receive funding from a wide range of sources, including donations and grants.

5. File the Application

- **Submit Form 1023 or 1023-EZ**: Mail Form 1023 to the IRS or submit Form 1023-EZ electronically. Along with the forms, you'll need to pay the application fee (currently $600 for Form 1023 and $275 for Form 1023-EZ).
- **Attach Supporting Documents**: Include your articles of incorporation, bylaws, financial statements, and any other required documentation.

6. Wait for IRS Approval

After submitting your application, the IRS will review it and decide whether to grant tax-exempt status. This process can take a few months, but if everything is in order, you should receive your determination letter.

7. Maintain Compliance

Once your church is granted 501(c)(3) status, there are several ongoing compliance requirements:

- **File Annual Returns**: File Form 990 or 990-N (e-Postcard) annually, depending on the church's size. Churches with annual gross receipts of $50,000 or less file the 990-N, while larger organizations may need to file Form 990 or 990-EZ.
- **Maintain Records**: Keep detailed records of donations, expenses, board meetings, and other church activities to ensure transparency and compliance with IRS regulations.

- **Avoid Political Activity**: Ensure that the church does not participate in political campaigns or lobbying beyond what is allowed for 501(c)(3) organizations.

2-STEP BY STEP CHARITY INVOLVES ORGANIZATION

Applying for 501(c)(3) status for a charity involves a detailed process with specific steps to ensure that the organization meets the IRS criteria for tax-exempt status. Below are the step-by-step instructions for charities applying for 501(c)(3) status:

1. Establish Your Charity as a Legal Entity

Before applying for 501(c)(3) status, your charity must be a legally established entity. This typically involves the following steps:

- **Choose a Name for Your Charity**: Make sure the name is not already in use by checking your state's business registry.
- **Draft Articles of Incorporation**: File these with your state's Secretary of State or similar agency. The articles must include language that specifies your charitable purpose and confirms that no part of the charity's earnings will benefit private individuals. This ensures the charity meets the IRS requirements.
- **Create Bylaws**: Bylaws define how your organization will operate, including the roles and responsibilities of board members, the decision-making process, and the structure of meetings.

2. Appoint a Board of Directors

You will need to appoint a board of directors or trustees to manage the charity. The board should consist of at least three members (depending on your state's requirements). The board is responsible for overseeing the organization's operations and ensuring it follows its mission.

3. Obtain an Employer Identification Number (EIN)

Apply for an EIN from the IRS. This number is necessary for filing taxes, opening a bank account, and applying for 501(c)(3) status.

- **How to Apply for EIN**: You can apply for an EIN online through the IRS website for free.

4. Ensure Your Charity Qualifies for 501(c)(3) Status

The IRS has strict rules for charities applying for tax-exempt status. Make sure your charity qualifies under the following guidelines:

- **Purpose**: The charity must operate exclusively for religious, charitable, educational, scientific, or literary purposes. This includes:
  - Relief of the poor, the distressed, or the underprivileged
  - Advancing education or science
  - Preventing cruelty to children or animals
  - Promoting the arts, among other purposes.
- **Public Benefit**: The charity must benefit the public, not private individuals.
- **No Private Inurement**: The charity's earnings should not benefit individuals or insiders, such as board members or officers.
- **No Political Campaigning or Excessive Lobbying**: Charities can advocate for policies but cannot engage in political campaigning or lobbying that could risk their 501(c)(3) status.

5. Prepare Form 1023 or Form 1023-EZ

The IRS offers two forms for applying for 501(c)(3) status:

- **Form 1023 (Long Form)**: This is the detailed application for tax-exempt status. It requires comprehensive information about the organization, including its structure, finances, governance, and activities.
- **Form 1023-EZ (Short Form)**: A simplified form for smaller organizations that meet specific criteria, including gross receipts of $50,000 or less and assets under $250,000.

Instructions for Completing Form 1023/1023-EZ:

- **Part I: Identification of Applicant**: Enter the charity's name, EIN, and address.

- **Part II: Organizational Structure**: Indicate whether the charity is a corporation, trust, or unincorporated association. You will need to submit copies of your articles of incorporation and bylaws.
- **Part III: Narrative Description of Activities**: Provide a detailed description of your charity's past, present, and planned activities. Be specific about how your programs will further your charitable purposes.
- **Part IV: Financial Data**: Provide financial statements, including projected income and expenses for the next three years if the charity is newly established. If your charity has been operating, you will need to provide financial data for the past few years.
- **Part V: Compensation and Insider Benefits**: Disclose any compensation paid to board members, officers, or key employees, ensuring that it is reasonable and does not violate the IRS's private inurement rules.
- **Part VI: Public Charity Status**: Confirm that your charity qualifies as a public charity, which means it is supported by the public (through donations, grants, etc.) rather than being a private foundation.

6. Submit the Application to the IRS

- **File Form 1023 or Form 1023-EZ**: If you are filing Form 1023, mail the completed application along with the required documentation and fee (currently $600) to the IRS. For Form 1023-EZ, you can submit it electronically through the IRS website for a fee of $275.
- **Attach Supporting Documents**: Include your articles of incorporation, bylaws, financial data, and any additional information requested by the IRS.

7. Wait for IRS Determination

After you submit your application, the IRS will review your submission and make a determination. The review process for Form 1023 can take 3-6 months, whereas Form 1023-EZ applications are usually processed faster, often within a few months.

- **Determination Letter**: If approved, you will receive an IRS determination letter that grants your charity 501(c)(3) status. This letter is critical for obtaining tax-deductible donations and grants.

8. Maintain Ongoing Compliance

Once your charity is granted 501(c)(3) status, it must follow IRS compliance rules to maintain its tax-exempt status:

- **Annual IRS Filings**: Most charities must file Form 990, 990-EZ, or 990-N (e-Postcard) annually. Small charities with gross receipts of $50,000 or less file the 990-N.
- **Maintain Records**: Keep detailed records of donations, expenses, board meetings, and other activities. This ensures transparency and compliance with IRS regulations.
- **Ongoing Charitable Purpose**: Continue operating exclusively for charitable purposes and avoid engaging in prohibited activities such as political campaigning or excessive lobbying.
- **Disclosure Requirements**: You must make your Form 1023 and Form 990 filings available to the public upon request.

9. Consider Additional State Requirements

While 501(c)(3) status is at the federal level, many states have their own requirements for charitable organizations. These may include:

- **State Charitable Solicitation Registration**: Some states require charities to register before soliciting donations.
- **State Tax Exemption**: If your charity operates in a state with income or sales tax, you may need to apply for state-level tax exemptions.

3-STEP BY STEP HOW TO START CHILDREN ORGANIZATION

To create a children's organization and apply for 501(c)(3) tax-exempt status, the process is similar to other nonprofits, but with a focus on child-related services. Below are the detailed step-by-step instructions for establishing a children's organization and obtaining 501(c)(3) status:

1. Define the Mission and Purpose of the Children's Organization

Before starting, clearly define the mission and purpose of your organization. Since it will be a children's organization, focus on how it will help children in areas such as:

- Education and literacy programs
- Health and wellness initiatives
- Providing food, clothing, or shelter
- Support for at-risk children, including orphans or children in foster care
- Recreational and after-school programs

Ensure your purpose meets IRS requirements for 501(c)(3) eligibility, which includes charitable, educational, and religious activities.

2. Formulate a Plan for the Organization's Activities

Create a detailed plan outlining the specific activities and programs your children's organization will offer. This plan should align with your mission and include:

- The types of services you'll provide (e.g., mentoring, tutoring, or providing resources to underprivileged children).
- Who will benefit (e.g., children from low-income families, children with disabilities, etc.).

- How your organization will operate (e.g., through partnerships, volunteers, and donors).

3. Establish the Legal Structure of the Organization

Your children's organization must be a legally recognized entity to apply for 501(c)(3) status. Here's how to establish your organization:

- **Choose a Name**: Select a unique name for your organization, ensuring it is not already in use.
- **Incorporate Your Organization**: File Articles of Incorporation with your state's Secretary of State or similar agency. Be sure to include language stating that the organization is organized exclusively for charitable purposes as required by the IRS.
  - You can often find templates for nonprofit incorporation documents from your state government or nonprofit associations.
- **Draft Bylaws**: Bylaws serve as the internal rules of your organization, explaining how it will be governed. Include details such as:
  - The responsibilities of board members and officers
  - Procedures for board meetings and decision-making
  - Conflict of interest policies (a requirement for 501(c)(3) status)

4. Appoint a Board of Directors

You will need to appoint a board of directors to oversee the children's organization. The board must consist of individuals who are not related by blood or marriage to avoid conflicts of interest.

- **Create Roles for Officers**: Assign roles like President, Treasurer, and Secretary to different individuals. These people will be responsible for overseeing the nonprofit's activities and making key decisions.

5. Obtain an Employer Identification Number (EIN)

You need an Employer Identification Number (EIN) to apply for tax-exempt status and to open a bank account.

- **How to Apply**: You can obtain an EIN for free through the IRS website.

6. Prepare to File for 501(c)(3) Tax-Exempt Status

You will now begin preparing the application to file for 501(c)(3) status with the IRS. To do so, you'll need to meet IRS qualifications, which include:

- Operating exclusively for charitable, educational, or religious purposes
- Having a public benefit, such as helping children in need
- No part of the organization's earnings benefiting private individuals (this is called private inurement)
- Restrictions on political activities and lobbying

7. Prepare IRS Form 1023 or 1023-EZ

You will need to complete either **Form 1023** (the long form) or **Form 1023-EZ** (the short form), depending on the size and complexity of your organization. Smaller organizations with projected annual revenues of less than $50,000 can apply using the 1023-EZ form.

Form 1023 (Long Form):

- **Part I**: Basic information, including your organization's name, EIN, and address.
- **Part II**: Organizational structure, including your articles of incorporation and bylaws.
- **Part III**: Narrative description of your children's organization's activities, including the programs and services you will provide for children.
- **Part IV**: Financial statements, including your projected income and expenses for the next three years (especially if your organization is new). If the organization has already been operating, include past financial records.
- **Part V**: Compensation and insider benefits—detail any compensation given to officers, directors, or key employees.

- **Part VI**: Public charity status—confirm that your organization will operate as a public charity, which receives its funding from the public rather than a private foundation.

Form 1023-EZ (Short Form):

- **Streamlined process** for smaller organizations, filed online. You will answer questions about your organization's activities, structure, and finances.

8. Submit the 501(c)(3) Application

- **Form 1023 or 1023-EZ**: Submit Form 1023 by mailing it to the IRS or filing Form 1023-EZ electronically. Be sure to include the application fee (currently $600 for Form 1023 and $275 for Form 1023-EZ).
- **Attach Supporting Documents**: Include your Articles of Incorporation, bylaws, and any financial records required by the IRS.

9. Wait for IRS Approval

After submission, the IRS will review your application and make a determination. This can take several months for Form 1023 and less time for Form 1023-EZ.

- **IRS Determination Letter**: If approved, you will receive an official IRS determination letter that confirms your organization is recognized as a 501(c)(3) tax-exempt charity. This status allows your organization to receive tax-deductible donations.

10. Comply with Ongoing IRS and State Regulations

Once your children's organization is granted 501(c)(3) status, you must comply with the following ongoing requirements:

- **Annual IRS Filings**: File Form 990, 990-EZ, or 990-N (e-Postcard) each year based on your organization's income level.
  - Charities with less than $50,000 in revenue can file the simpler Form 990-N.

- **Maintain Records**: Keep detailed financial records, including receipts of donations, expenses, and board meeting minutes.
- **Public Charity Operations**: Ensure that your organization continues to operate exclusively for charitable purposes and does not engage in political campaigning or excessive lobbying.

11. State-Level Compliance and Charitable Solicitations

- **State Registration**: Depending on your state, you may need to register to solicit donations. Many states require charities to register before they can legally solicit donations from the public.
- **State Tax Exemption**: If your state has income or sales taxes, you may also need to apply for a state-level tax exemption.

4-INTERNATIONAL NONPROFIT

Opening an international nonprofit organization involves several steps, including defining your mission, setting up your legal structure, and ensuring compliance with both U.S. and international regulations. Here's a step-by-step guide to help you launch an international nonprofit organization and apply for 501(c)(3) status in the U.S., if applicable.

Step 1: Define the Mission and Scope of Your International Nonprofit

- **Clarify your mission**: Define what issue or cause your organization will address internationally, such as education, poverty alleviation, health services, human rights, etc.
- **Target Countries**: Identify the countries or regions where you plan to operate and the specific populations you intend to serve.
- **Program and Services**: Define what types of programs or services you will provide to fulfill your mission. For example, will you focus on building schools, providing healthcare, or advocacy work?

Step 2: Research Legal Requirements in the U.S. and Target Countries

- **U.S. Requirements**: If you're planning to operate from the U.S. and seek tax-exempt status, you will follow U.S. nonprofit laws, including applying for 501(c)(3) status.
- **Foreign Regulations**: Research the legal and regulatory requirements of the countries where you plan to operate. Many countries have rules regarding foreign NGOs (Non-Governmental Organizations) or nonprofits, and you may need to register locally.
- **International Laws**: Ensure that your nonprofit will comply with international laws and treaties, especially if you're engaging in activities like disaster relief or cross-border aid.

Step 3: Establish Your Nonprofit as a Legal Entity

1. **Choose a Name**: Select a unique name for your organization, ensuring it reflects your mission and is not already in use.
2. **Draft Articles of Incorporation**: File your Articles of Incorporation with your state (in the U.S.) or in the country where you are based. These articles should include:
   - The name and purpose of the organization (focused on charitable or educational goals).
   - A clear statement that your organization will not engage in political or lobbying activities (important for U.S. 501(c)(3) eligibility).
   - A dissolution clause stating that any remaining assets will be distributed to another 501(c)(3) organization upon dissolution.
3. **Create Bylaws**: Draft bylaws that outline how your organization will operate, including:
   - Board governance (how many board members you'll have and their responsibilities).
   - How board members are selected or replaced.
   - Procedures for holding meetings and making decisions.

Step 4: Form a Board of Directors

A nonprofit organization requires a board of directors to oversee its operations and ensure accountability. Choose a diverse group of individuals committed to the mission of the organization, and make sure there is no conflict of interest (e.g., board members should not be family members).

Step 5: Obtain an Employer Identification Number (EIN)

Apply for an EIN from the IRS, which is like a social security number for your nonprofit organization. This is required for tax purposes and for setting up a bank account. You can apply online for free through the IRS website.

Step 6: Determine If You Will Apply for 501(c)(3) Status

If you plan to seek U.S. tax-exempt status, you will need to apply for 501(c)(3) status with the IRS. This status allows you to:

- Offer tax deductions to U.S. donors.
- Apply for grants and other funding from U.S.-based organizations.

Steps to Apply for 501(c) (3) Status:

1. **Prepare Form 1023 or Form 1023-EZ**:
   - **Form 1023**: This is the full application for tax-exempt status. It requires detailed information about your organization's activities, structure, and finances.
   - **Form 1023-EZ**: A simpler application for smaller organizations with annual gross receipts of $50,000 or less.
2. **Complete the Application**:
   - Provide a description of your international programs, how they will further your charitable purpose, and the countries in which you'll operate.
   - Include financial data such as projected budgets and sources of funding.
   - Submit supporting documents such as Articles of Incorporation and bylaws.
3. **Submit the Application**: File your Form 1023 (or 1023-EZ) with the IRS along with the application fee. Form 1023 costs $600, and Form 1023-EZ costs $275.

Step 7: Establish Financial and Fundraising Strategies

1. **Open a Bank Account**: Once you receive your EIN, open a bank account in your organization's name.
2. **Set Up Accounting Systems**: Use accounting software or hire an accountant familiar with nonprofit accounting to help track donations, expenses, and other financial information.
3. **Fundraising Plans**:

- Develop a strategy to raise funds both domestically and internationally. This can include grants, donations, fundraising events, and corporate sponsorships.
- Ensure that you comply with any fundraising regulations in the U.S. and other countries where you operate.

Step 8: Register in Other Countries Where You Will Operate

- **Local Registration**: In most cases, you will need to register your nonprofit as a legal entity in the countries where you plan to operate. Each country has different rules for how foreign nonprofits can register and operate. Make sure to comply with their laws and maintain transparency to avoid issues.
- **Partnerships**: Consider partnering with local organizations or NGOs that are already established in the countries where you will operate. This can help you navigate local regulations and gain credibility.

Step 9: Develop Your Programs and Operations

1. **Build Partnerships**: Establish partnerships with local governments, NGOs, and communities in the countries you will serve.
2. **Hire Staff and Volunteers**: If your operations are large, consider hiring staff members both in your home country and in the countries where you will operate. You can also recruit local volunteers who understand the community's needs.
3. **Create Clear Program Plans**: Ensure that your programs have clear goals, timelines, and measurable outcomes. Regularly assess the impact of your programs to ensure you are fulfilling your mission.
4. **Ensure Legal Compliance**: Follow both U.S. and international regulations regarding employment, taxes, and reporting. For example, some countries may require local financial reporting, while the IRS requires you to file Form 990 annually to maintain 501(c)(3) status.

Step 10: Maintain Ongoing Compliance

- **Annual IRS Filing (Form 990)**: If your nonprofit is based in the U.S. and has 501(c)(3) status, you must file an annual Form 990 with the IRS. This form provides transparency on your nonprofit's finances and activities.
- **Country-Specific Reporting**: In the countries where you operate, ensure you file any required reports to the local government, such as financial audits or impact reports.
- **Recordkeeping**: Maintain thorough records of your operations, including donor contributions, program expenditures, and board meeting minutes.

Step 11: Build a Global Network and Outreach

- **Online Presence**: Develop a website and social media accounts to promote your mission and reach a global audience. Offer opportunities for donations, volunteering, and partnerships.
- **Global Networking**: Join international nonprofit associations or attend conferences that can help you connect with other organizations, donors, and government agencies.

Step 12: Apply for Grants and Funding

Many international organizations rely on grants from foundations, government agencies, and international bodies like the United Nations or World Bank. Research available grants that align with your mission and apply for funding to sustain your programs.

SAMPLE LETTER FOR REQUEST FOR DONATION

[Your Organization's Letterhead]

[Date]

[Donor's Name or Business Name]
[Donor's Address]
[City, State, ZIP Code]

Dear **[Donor's Name]**,

I hope this letter finds you well. My name is **[Your Name]**, and I am writing on behalf of **[Your Organization's Name]**, a nonprofit organization dedicated to **[briefly describe your mission, e.g., supporting women, helping children, providing educational resources, etc.]**. We are excited to announce our upcoming event, **[Name of the Event]**, which will be held on **[Date]** at **[Location]**.

[Name of the Event] is a special initiative designed to **[purpose of the event, e.g., raise funds for a new community program, support educational activities, provide resources for underprivileged children, etc.]**. With this event, we aim to **[specific goal, such as distribute food to 500 families, raise $10,000, provide scholarships, etc.]**, and we are confident it will have a significant impact on the community.

We are reaching out to you because **[Donor's Name or Business Name]** has a strong reputation for supporting causes like ours, and we believe you share our passion for **[insert relevant cause, e.g., improving the lives of children, helping families in need, etc.]**. To make this event a success, we are seeking generous donations to help cover **[list specific needs: event supplies, food, shelter, educational materials, etc.]**.

Your contribution will directly help us achieve our goal of **[describe what their donation will support, e.g., providing meals to 200 families, supporting women**

in crisis, offering school supplies to children, etc.]. Any amount you can give will make a difference and bring us one step closer to making this event a success.

In recognition of your generous donation, we would be honored to **[mention any recognition or benefits: include your logo on event materials, give a shoutout on social media, or offer VIP tickets to the event, etc.].**

We would be happy to provide more information about **[Your Organization's Name]** and our event. Please feel free to contact me at **[Your Phone Number]** or **[Your Email Address]** if you have any questions or need additional details.

Thank you for considering our request. Together, we can make a real difference in the lives of those we serve. We hope that you will join us in supporting **[Name of the Event]** and our mission to **[restating the mission briefly].**

Warm regards,

[Your Name]
[Your Title]
[Your Organization's Name]
[Your Contact Information]
[Website URL]

SAMPLE LETTER FOR GRANT APPLICATION

[Your Organization's Letterhead]
[Date]

[Grant Provider's Name]
[Organization's Name]
[Address]
[City, State, ZIP Code]

Dear **[Grant Provider's Name or Review Committee]**,

I hope this letter finds you well. On behalf of **[Your Organization's Name]**, I am writing to respectfully request consideration for a grant to support our **[specific program or project]**. We are a **[briefly describe your organization, e.g., nonprofit organization dedicated to supporting women in need, children's education, environmental conservation, etc.]**, and our mission is to **[state your organization's mission statement]**.

We are seeking a grant in the amount of **[specific amount requested]** to help fund **[describe the program or project that will be funded]**. This project is focused on **[explain the goal of the project, e.g., providing educational resources to underprivileged children, building safe shelters for homeless families, offering skills training for women, etc.]**. With the financial support of **[grant provider's name or organization]**, we will be able to **[describe the specific impact of the grant, e.g., reach 500 children, offer 100 families assistance, reduce the carbon footprint in our community, etc.]**.

[Provide background and statistics, if applicable. For example: "Currently, over 40% of children in our region do not have access to quality educational resources. Through our program, we aim to close this gap by providing books, tutoring, and mentorship programs to children in underserved communities."]

[Your Organization's Name] has a proven track record of successfully executing impactful programs, such as **[mention any previous achievements, projects, or partnerships, if applicable]**. We are confident that, with your support, we can achieve the goals outlined in this proposal and create lasting change in the community.

We have attached a detailed proposal, including a budget and timeline, for your review. Should you require any additional information or have any questions, please feel free to contact me directly at **[Your Phone Number]** or **[Your Email Address]**.

We sincerely appreciate your time and consideration of our request. We are excited about the possibility of partnering with **[grant provider's name]** to make a significant impact through **[project/program name]**. Your support will make an incredible difference in the lives of **[the population or cause you are serving, e.g., at-risk youth, women in crisis, environmental sustainability efforts]**.

Thank you again for your consideration.

Warm regards,

[Your Name]
[Your Title]
[Your Organization's Name]
[Your Contact Information]
[Website URL]

SAMPLE LETTER

[Your Name]
Founder,
[Your Address]
[City, State, Zip Code]
[Phone Number]
[Email Address]
[Date]

[Sponsor's Name]
[Their Title]
[Company Name]
[Company Address]
[City, State, Zip Code]

Dear [Sponsor's Name],

I hope this letter finds you well. My name is [Your Name], and I am the founder of
, a nonprofit organization dedicated to empowering and supporting women in need, including survivors of abuse, single mothers, and refugee women. We provide crucial assistance by helping women secure shelter, find employment, and build strong resumes to restart their lives.

For over two years, has been an active force in our community, offering valuable resources to help women build sustainable futures. We've hosted toy giveaways for children and provided school supplies to families in need. In our latest effort, we plan to give away this Thanksgiving to families who otherwise may not have a meal to celebrate the holiday.

To continue our mission, we rely on the generous support of community partners like you. We are reaching out to ask if [Company Name] would consider sponsoring our organization. Your sponsorship would help us extend our reach to more women and families, providing essential services at no cost to those who need them most.

As a sponsor, your business would be acknowledged on our website, social media, and at our community events. This is a wonderful opportunity to align your brand with a cause that directly impacts the lives of women and families in our local community.

We are happy to provide further details on sponsorship packages or discuss other ways [Company Name] can support our efforts. Thank you for considering our request. Your support will make a tremendous difference in the lives of many.

I would be grateful for the opportunity to speak with you directly. Please feel free to reach me at [Phone Number] or [Email Address].

Warm regards,

[Your Name]
Founder,
[Phone Number]
[Email Address]

Form **1023-EZ**

(June 2014)

Department of the Treasury
Internal Revenue Service

Streamlined Application for Recognition of Exemption Under Section 501(c)(3) of the Internal Revenue Code

▶ **Do not enter social security numbers on this form as it may be made public.**
▶ Information about Form 1023-EZ and its separate instructions is at *www.irs.gov/form1023.*

OMB No. 1545-0056

Note: *If exempt status is approved, this application will be open for public inspection.*

☐ Check this box to attest that you have completed the Form 1023-EZ Eligibility Worksheet in the current instructions, are eligible to apply for exemption using Form 1023-EZ, and have read and understand the requirements to be exempt under section 501(c)(3).

Part I — Identification of Applicant

1a Full Name of Organization

b Address (number, street, and room/suite). If a P.O. box, see instructions. **c** City **d** State **e** Zip Code + 4

2 Employer Identification Number **3** Month Tax Year Ends (MM) **4** Person to Contact if More Information is Needed

5 Contact Telephone Number **6** Fax Number (optional) **7** User Fee Submitted

8 List the names, titles, and mailing addresses of your officers, directors, and/or trustees. (If you have more than five, see instructions.)

First Name:	Last Name:	Title:	
Street Address:	City:	State:	Zip Code + 4:
First Name:	Last Name:	Title:	
Street Address:	City:	State:	Zip Code + 4:
First Name:	Last Name:	Title:	
Street Address:	City:	State:	Zip Code + 4:
First Name:	Last Name:	Title:	
Street Address:	City:	State:	Zip Code + 4:
First Name:	Last Name:	Title:	
Street Address:	City:	State:	Zip Code + 4:

9 a Organization's Website (if available):
b Organization's Email (optional):

Part II — Organizational Structure

1 To file this form, you must be a corporation, an unincorporated association, or a trust. **Check the box** for the type of organization.
☐ Corporation ☑ Unincorporated association ☐ Trust

2 ☐ **Check this box** to attest that you have the organizing document necessary for the organizational structure indicated above. (See the instructions for an explanation of **necessary organizing documents**.)

3 Date incorporated if a corporation, or formed if other than a corporation (MMDDYYYY): _____

4 State of incorporation or other formation: _____

5 Section 501(c)(3) requires that your organizing document must limit your purposes to one or more exempt purposes within section 501(c)(3).
☐ **Check this box** to attest that your organizing document contains this limitation.

6 Section 501(c)(3) requires that your organizing document must not expressly empower you to engage, otherwise than as an insubstantial part of your activities, in activities that in themselves are not in furtherance of one or more exempt purposes.

☐ **Check this box** to attest that your organizing document does not expressly empower you to engage, otherwise than as an insubstantial part of your activities, in activities that in themselves are not in furtherance of one or more exempt purposes.

7 Section 501(c)(3) requires that your organizing document must provide that upon dissolution, your remaining assets be used exclusively for section 501(c)(3) exempt purposes. Depending on your entity type and the state in which you are formed, this requirement may be satisfied by operation of state law.

☐ **Check this box** to attest that your organizing document contains the dissolution provision required under section 501(c)(3) or that you do not need an express dissolution provision in your organizing document because you rely on the operation of state law in the state in which you are formed for your dissolution provision.

For Paperwork Reduction Act Notice, see the instructions. Catalog No. 66267N Form **1023-EZ** (6-2014)

Part III   Your Specific Activities

1   Enter the appropriate 3-character NTEE Code that best describes your activities (See the instructions): _____

2   To qualify for exemption as a section 501(c)(3) organization, you must be organized and operated exclusively to further one or more of the following purposes. By checking the box or boxes below, you attest that you are organized and operated exclusively to further the purposes indicated. **Check all that apply.**

☐ Charitable   ☐ Religious   ☐ Educational

☐ Scientific   ☐ Literary   ☐ Testing for public safety

☐ To foster national or international amateur sports competition   ☐ Prevention of cruelty to children or animals

3   To qualify for exemption as a section 501(c)(3) organization, you must:

- Refrain from supporting or opposing candidates in political campaigns in any way.
- Ensure that your net earnings do not inure in whole or in part to the benefit of private shareholders or individuals (that is, board members, officers, key management employees, or other insiders).
- Not further non-exempt purposes (such as purposes that benefit private interests) more than insubstantially.
- Not be organized or operated for the primary purpose of conducting a trade or business that is not related to your exempt purpose(s).
- Not devote more than an insubstantial part of your activities attempting to influence legislation or, if you made a section 501(h) election, not normally make expenditures in excess of expenditure limitations outlined in section 501(h).
- Not provide commercial-type insurance as a substantial part of your activities.

☐ **Check this box** to attest that you have not conducted and will not conduct activities that violate these prohibitions and restrictions.

4   Do you or will you attempt to influence legislation? . . . . ☐ Yes ☐ No

     (If yes, consider filing Form 5768. See the instructions for more details.)

5   Do you or will you pay compensation to any of your officers, directors, or trustees? . . . . ☐ Yes ☐ No

     (Refer to the instructions for a definition of **compensation.**)

6   Do you or will you donate funds to or pay expenses for individual(s)? . . . . ☐ Yes ☐ No

7   Do you or will you conduct activities or provide grants or other assistance to individual(s) or organization(s) outside the United States? . . . . ☐ Yes ☐ No

8   Do you or will you engage in financial transactions (for example, loans, payments, rents, etc.) with any of your officers, directors, or trustees, or any entities they own or control? . . . . ☐ Yes ☐ No

9   Do you or will you have unrelated business gross income of $1,000 or more during a tax year? . . . . ☐ Yes ☐ No

10   Do you or will you operate bingo or other gaming activities? . . . . ☐ Yes ☐ No

11   Do you or will you provide disaster relief? . . . . ☐ Yes ☐ No

Part IV   Foundation Classification

Part IV is designed to classify you as an organization that is either a private foundation or a public charity. Public charity status is a more favorable tax status than private foundation status.

1   If you qualify for public charity status, check the appropriate box (**1a – 1c** below) and skip to **Part V** below.

   a ☐   **Check this box** to attest that you normally receive at least one-third of your support from public sources or you normally receive at least 10 percent of your support from public sources and you have other characteristics of a publicly supported organization. **Sections 509(a)(1) and 170(b)(1)(A)(vi).**

   b ☐   **Check this box** to attest that you normally receive more than one-third of your support from a combination of gifts, grants, contributions, membership fees, and gross receipts (from permitted sources) from activities related to your exempt functions and normally receive not more than one-third of your support from investment income and unrelated business taxable income. **Section 509(a)(2).**

   c ☐   **Check this box** to attest that you are operated for the benefit of a college or university that is owned or operated by a governmental unit. **Sections 509(a)(1) and 170(b)(1)(A)(iv).**

2   If you are not described in items **1a – 1c** above, you are a private foundation. As a private foundation, you are required by section 508(e) to have specific provisions in your organizing document, unless you rely on the operation of state law in the state in which you were formed to meet these requirements. These specific provisions require that you operate to avoid liability for private foundation excise taxes under sections 4941-4945.

    ☐   **Check this box** to attest that your organizing document contains the provisions required by section 508(e) or that your organizing document does not need to include the provisions required by section 508(e) because you rely on the operation of state law in your particular state to meet the requirements of section 508(e). (See the instructions for explanation of the section 508(e) requirements.)

Form **1023-EZ** (6-2014)

Form 1023-EZ (6-2014)   Page **3**

Part V — Reinstatement After Automatic Revocation

Complete this section only if you are applying for reinstatement of exemption after being automatically revoked for failure to file required annual returns or notices for three consecutive years, and you are applying for reinstatement under section 4 or 7 of Revenue Procedure 2014-11. (Check only one box.)

1 ☐ **Check this box** if you are seeking retroactive reinstatement under section 4 of Revenue Procedure 2014-11. By checking this box, you attest that you meet the specified requirements of section 4, that your failure to file was not intentional, and that you have put in place procedures to file required returns or notices in the future. (See the instructions for requirements.)

2 ☐ **Check this box** if you are seeking reinstatement under section 7 of Revenue Procedure 2014-11, effective the date you are filing this application.

Part VI — Signature

☐ I declare under the penalties of perjury that I am authorized to sign this application on behalf of the above organization and that I have examined this application, and to the best of my knowledge it is true, correct, and complete.

_____   _____
(Type name of signer)   (Type title or authority of signer)

**PLEASE
SIGN
HERE**
▶ _____   ▶ _____
(Signature of Officer, Director, Trustee, or other authorized official)   (Date)

Form **1023-EZ** (6-2014)

♻ *Printed on recycled paper*

Form **1023**

(Rev. December 2017)
Department of the Treasury
Internal Revenue Service

Application for Recognition of Exemption
Under Section 501(c)(3) of the Internal Revenue Code

▶ Do not enter social security numbers on this form as it may be made public.
▶ Go to *www.irs.gov/Form1023* for instructions and the latest information.

OMB No. 1545-0056

Note: If exempt status is approved, this application will be open for public inspection.

*Use the instructions to complete this application and for a definition of all **bold** items. For additional help, call IRS Exempt Organizations Customer Account Services toll-free at 1-877-829-5500. Visit our website at **www.irs.gov** for forms and publications. If the required information and documents are not submitted with payment of the appropriate user fee, the application may be returned to you.*

Attach additional sheets to this application if you need more space to answer fully. Put your name and EIN on each sheet and identify each answer by Part and line number. Complete Parts I – XI of Form 1023 and submit only those Schedules (A through H) that apply to you.

Part I	Identification of Applicant

1 Full name of organization (exactly as it appears in your **organizing document**)

2 c/o Name (if applicable)

3 **Mailing address** (Number and street) (see instructions) | Room/Suite

4 Employer Identification Number (EIN)

City or town, state or country, and ZIP + 4

5 Month the annual accounting period ends (01 – 12)

6 Primary contact (officer, director, trustee, or **authorized representative**)
a Name:

b Phone:

c Fax: (optional)

7 Are you represented by an authorized representative, such as an attorney or accountant? If "Yes," provide the authorized representative's name, and the name and address of the authorized representative's firm. Include a completed Form 2848, *Power of Attorney and Declaration of Representative*, with your application if you would like us to communicate with your representative. ☐ Yes ☐ No

8 Was a person who is not one of your officers, directors, trustees, employees, or an authorized representative listed in line 7, paid, or promised payment, to help plan, manage, or advise you about the structure or activities of your organization, or about your financial or tax matters? If "Yes," provide the person's name, the name and address of the person's firm, the amounts paid or promised to be paid, and describe that person's role. ☐ Yes ☐ No

9a Organization's website:

b Organization's email: (optional)

10 Certain organizations are not required to file an information return (Form 990 or Form 990-EZ). If you are granted tax-exemption, are you claiming to be excused from filing Form 990 or Form 990-EZ? If "Yes," explain. See the instructions for a description of organizations not required to file Form 990 or Form 990-EZ. ☐ Yes ☐ No

11 Date incorporated if a corporation, or formed, if other than a corporation. (MM/DD/YYYY) / /

12 Were you formed under the laws of a **foreign country**? If "Yes," state the country. ☐ Yes ☐ No

For Paperwork Reduction Act Notice, see instructions. | Cat. No. 17133K | Form **1023** (Rev. 12-2017)

Part II   Organizational Structure

You must be a corporation (including a limited liability company), an unincorporated association, or a trust to be tax exempt. See instructions. **DO NOT file this form unless you can check "Yes" on lines 1, 2, 3, or 4.**

1	Are you a **corporation**? If "Yes," attach a copy of your articles of incorporation showing **certification of filing** with the appropriate state agency. Include copies of any amendments to your articles and be sure they also show state filing certification.	☐ Yes	☐ No
2	Are you a **limited liability company (LLC)**? If "Yes," attach a copy of your articles of organization showing certification of filing with the appropriate state agency. Also, if you adopted an operating agreement, attach a copy. Include copies of any amendments to your articles and be sure they show state filing certification. Refer to the instructions for circumstances when an LLC should not file its own exemption application.	☐ Yes	☐ No
3	Are you an **unincorporated association**? If "Yes," attach a copy of your articles of association, constitution, or other similar organizing document that is dated and includes at least two signatures. Include signed and dated copies of any amendments.	☐ Yes	☐ No
4a	Are you a **trust**? If "Yes," attach a signed and dated copy of your trust agreement. Include signed and dated copies of any amendments.	☐ Yes	☐ No
b	Have you been funded? If "No," explain how you are formed without anything of value placed in trust.	☐ Yes	☐ No
5	Have you adopted **bylaws**? If "Yes," attach a current copy showing date of adoption. If "No," explain how your officers, directors, or trustees are selected.	☐ Yes	☐ No

Part III   Required Provisions in Your Organizing Document

The following questions are designed to ensure that when you file this application, your organizing document contains the required provisions to meet the organizational test under section 501(c)(3). Unless you can check the boxes in both lines 1 and 2, your organizing document does not meet the organizational test. **DO NOT file this application until you have amended your organizing document.** Submit your original and amended organizing documents (showing state filing certification if you are a corporation or an LLC) with your application.

1	Section 501(c)(3) requires that your organizing document state your exempt purpose(s), such as charitable, religious, educational, and/or scientific purposes. Check the box to confirm that your organizing document meets this requirement. Describe specifically where your organizing document meets this requirement, such as a reference to a particular article or section in your organizing document. Refer to the instructions for exempt purpose language.	☐

Location of Purpose Clause (Page, Article, and Paragraph):

2a	Section 501(c)(3) requires that upon dissolution of your organization, your remaining assets must be used exclusively for exempt purposes, such as charitable, religious, educational, and/or scientific purposes. Check the box on line 2a to confirm that your organizing document meets this requirement by express provision for the distribution of assets upon dissolution. If you rely on state law for your dissolution provision, do not check the box on line 2a and go to line 2c.	☐
b	If you checked the box on line 2a, specify the location of your dissolution clause (Page, Article, and Paragraph). Do not complete line 2c if you checked box 2a.	
c	See the instructions for information about the operation of state law in your particular state. Check this box if you rely on operation of state law for your dissolution provision and indicate the state:	☐

Part IV   Narrative Description of Your Activities

Using an attachment, describe your *past*, *present*, and *planned* activities in a narrative. If you believe that you have already provided some of this information in response to other parts of this application, you may summarize that information here and refer to the specific parts of the application for supporting details. You may also attach representative copies of newsletters, brochures, or similar documents for supporting details to this narrative. Remember that if this application is approved, it will be open for public inspection. Therefore, your narrative description of activities should be thorough and accurate. Refer to the instructions for information that must be included in your description.

Part V   Compensation and Other Financial Arrangements With Your Officers, Directors, Trustees, Employees, and Independent Contractors

1a List the names, titles, and mailing addresses of all of your officers, directors, and trustees. For each person listed, state their total annual **compensation**, or proposed compensation, for all services to the organization, whether as an officer, employee, or other position. Use actual figures, if available. Enter "none" if no compensation is or will be paid. If additional space is needed, attach a separate sheet. Refer to the instructions for information on what to include as compensation.

Name	Title	Mailing address	Compensation amount (annual actual or estimated)

Part V	Compensation and Other Financial Arrangements With Your Officers, Directors, Trustees, Employees, and Independent Contractors *(Continued)*

b List the names, titles, and mailing addresses of each of your five highest compensated employees who receive or will receive compensation of more than $50,000 per year. Use the actual figure, if available. Refer to the instructions for information on what to include as compensation. Do not include officers, directors, or trustees listed in line 1a.

Name	Title	Mailing address	Compensation amount (annual actual or estimated)

c List the names, names of businesses, and mailing addresses of your five highest compensated **independent contractors** that receive or will receive compensation of more than $50,000 per year. Use the actual figure, if available. Refer to the instructions for information on what to include as compensation.

Name	Title	Mailing address	Compensation amount (annual actual or estimated)

The following "Yes" or "No" questions relate to *past, present,* or *planned* relationships, transactions, or agreements with your officers, directors, trustees, highest compensated employees, and highest compensated independent contractors listed in lines 1a, 1b, and 1c.

2a Are any of your officers, directors, or trustees **related** to each other through **family** or **business** **relationships**? If "Yes," identify the individuals and explain the relationship. ☐ Yes ☐ No

b Do you have a business relationship with any of your officers, directors, or trustees other than through their position as an officer, director, or trustee? If "Yes," identify the individuals and describe the business relationship with each of your officers, directors, or trustees. ☐ Yes ☐ No

c Are any of your officers, directors, or trustees related to your highest compensated employees or highest compensated independent contractors listed on lines 1b or 1c through family or business relationships? If "Yes," identify the individuals and explain the relationship. ☐ Yes ☐ No

3a For each of your officers, directors, trustees, highest compensated employees, and highest compensated independent contractors listed on lines 1a, 1b, or 1c, attach a list showing their name, qualifications, average hours worked, and duties.

b Do any of your officers, directors, trustees, highest compensated employees, and highest compensated independent contractors listed on lines 1a, 1b, or 1c receive compensation from any other organizations, whether tax exempt or taxable, that are related to you through **common control**? If "Yes," identify the individuals, explain the relationship between you and the other organization, and describe the compensation arrangement. ☐ Yes ☐ No

4 In establishing the compensation for your officers, directors, trustees, highest compensated employees, and highest compensated independent contractors listed on lines 1a, 1b, and 1c, the following practices are recommended, although they are not required to obtain exemption. Answer "Yes" to all the practices you use.

a Do you or will the individuals that approve compensation arrangements follow a conflict of interest policy? ☐ Yes ☐ No

b Do you or will you approve compensation arrangements in advance of paying compensation? ☐ Yes ☐ No

c Do you or will you document in writing the date and terms of approved compensation arrangements? ☐ Yes ☐ No

Form **1023** (Rev. 12-2017)

| **Part V** | Compensation and Other Financial Arrangements With Your Officers, Directors, Trustees, Employees, and Independent Contractors *(Continued)* |

d Do you or will you record in writing the decision made by each individual who decided or voted on compensation arrangements? ☐ Yes ☐ No

e Do you or will you approve compensation arrangements based on information about compensation paid by **similarly situated** taxable or tax-exempt organizations for similar services, current compensation surveys compiled by independent firms, or actual written offers from similarly situated organizations? Refer to the Instructions for Part V, lines 1a, 1b, and 1c, for information on what to include as compensation. ☐ Yes ☐ No

f Do you or will you record in writing both the information on which you relied to base your decision and its source? ☐ Yes ☐ No

g If you answered "No" to any item on lines 4a through 4f, describe how you set compensation that is **reasonable** for your officers, directors, trustees, highest compensated employees, and highest compensated independent contractors listed in Part V, lines 1a, 1b, and 1c.

5a Have you adopted a **conflict of interest policy** consistent with the sample conflict of interest policy in Appendix A to the instructions? If "Yes," provide a copy of the policy and explain how the policy has been adopted, such as by resolution of your governing board. If "No," answer lines 5b and 5c. ☐ Yes ☐ No

b What procedures will you follow to assure that persons who have a conflict of interest will not have influence over you for setting their own compensation?

c What procedures will you follow to assure that persons who have a conflict of interest will not have influence over you regarding business deals with themselves?
   Note: A conflict of interest policy is recommended though it is not required to obtain exemption. Hospitals, see Schedule C, Section I, line 14.

6a Do you or will you compensate any of your officers, directors, trustees, highest compensated employees, and highest compensated independent contractors listed in lines 1a, 1b, or 1c through **non-fixed payments**, such as discretionary bonuses or revenue-based payments? If "Yes," describe all non-fixed compensation arrangements, including how the amounts are determined, who is eligible for such arrangements, whether you place a limitation on total compensation, and how you determine or will determine that you pay no more than reasonable compensation for services. Refer to the instructions for Part V, lines 1a, 1b, and 1c, for information on what to include as compensation. ☐ Yes ☐ No

b Do you or will you compensate any of your employees, other than your officers, directors, trustees, or your five highest compensated employees who receive or will receive compensation of more than $50,000 per year, through non-fixed payments, such as discretionary bonuses or revenue-based payments? If "Yes," describe all non-fixed compensation arrangements, including how the amounts are or will be determined, who is or will be eligible for such arrangements, whether you place or will place a limitation on total compensation, and how you determine or will determine that you pay no more than reasonable compensation for services. Refer to the instructions for Part V, lines 1a, 1b, and 1c, for information on what to include as compensation. ☐ Yes ☐ No

7a Do you or will you purchase any goods, services, or assets from any of your officers, directors, trustees, highest compensated employees, or highest compensated independent contractors listed in lines 1a, 1b, or 1c? If "Yes," describe any such purchase that you made or intend to make, from whom you make or will make such purchases, how the terms are or will be negotiated at **arm's length**, and explain how you determine or will determine that you pay no more than **fair market value**. Attach copies of any written contracts or other agreements relating to such purchases. ☐ Yes ☐ No

b Do you or will you sell any goods, services, or assets to any of your officers, directors, trustees, highest compensated employees, or highest compensated independent contractors listed in lines 1a, 1b, or 1c? If "Yes," describe any such sales that you made or intend to make, to whom you make or will make such sales, how the terms are or will be negotiated at arm's length, and explain how you determine or will determine you are or will be paid at least fair market value. Attach copies of any written contracts or other agreements relating to such sales. ☐ Yes ☐ No

8a Do you or will you have any leases, contracts, loans, or other agreements with your officers, directors, trustees, highest compensated employees, or highest compensated independent contractors listed in lines 1a, 1b, or 1c? If "Yes," provide the information requested in lines 8b through 8f. ☐ Yes ☐ No

b Describe any written or oral arrangements that you made or intend to make.

c Identify with whom you have or will have such arrangements.

d Explain how the terms are or will be negotiated at arm's length.

e Explain how you determine you pay no more than fair market value or you are paid at least fair market value.

f Attach copies of any signed leases, contracts, loans, or other agreements relating to such arrangements.

9a Do you or will you have any leases, contracts, loans, or other agreements with any organization in which any of your officers, directors, or trustees are also officers, directors, or trustees, or in which any individual officer, director, or trustee owns more than a 35% interest? If "Yes," provide the information requested in lines 9b through 9f. ☐ Yes ☐ No

Form **1023** (Rev. 12-2017)

| Part V | Compensation and Other Financial Arrangements With Your Officers, Directors, Trustees, Employees, and Independent Contractors *(Continued)* |

b Describe any written or oral arrangements you made or intend to make.

c Identify with whom you have or will have such arrangements.

d Explain how the terms are or will be negotiated at arm's length.

e Explain how you determine or will determine you pay no more than fair market value or that you are paid at least fair market value.

f Attach a copy of any signed leases, contracts, loans, or other agreements relating to such arrangements.

| Part VI | Your Members and Other Individuals and Organizations That Receive Benefits From You |

The following "Yes" or "No" questions relate to goods, services, and funds you provide to individuals and organizations as part of your activities. Your answers should pertain to *past, present,* and *planned* activities. See instructions.

1a In carrying out your exempt purposes, do you provide goods, services, or funds to individuals? If "Yes," describe each program that provides goods, services, or funds to individuals. ☐ **Yes** ☐ **No**

b In carrying out your exempt purposes, do you provide goods, services, or funds to organizations? If "Yes," describe each program that provides goods, services, or funds to organizations. ☐ **Yes** ☐ **No**

2 Do any of your programs limit the provision of goods, services, or funds to a specific individual or group of specific individuals? For example, answer "Yes," if goods, services, or funds are provided only for a particular individual, your members, individuals who work for a particular employer, or graduates of a particular school. If "Yes," explain the limitation and how recipients are selected for each program. ☐ **Yes** ☐ **No**

3 Do any individuals who receive goods, services, or funds through your programs have a family or business relationship with any officer, director, trustee, or with any of your highest compensated employees or highest compensated independent contractors listed in Part V, lines 1a, 1b, and 1c? If "Yes," explain how these related individuals are eligible for goods, services, or funds. ☐ **Yes** ☐ **No**

| Part VII | Your History |

The following "Yes" or "No" questions relate to your history. See instructions.

1 Are you a **successor** to another organization? Answer "Yes," if you have taken or will take over the activities of another organization; you took over 25% or more of the fair market value of the net assets of another organization; or you were established upon the conversion of an organization from for-profit to nonprofit status. If "Yes," complete Schedule G. ☐ **Yes** ☐ **No**

2 Are you submitting this application more than 27 months after the end of the month in which you were legally formed? If "Yes," complete Schedule E. ☐ **Yes** ☐ **No**

| Part VIII | Your Specific Activities |

The following "Yes" or "No" questions relate to specific activities that you may conduct. Check the appropriate box. Your answers should pertain to *past, present,* and *planned* activities. See instructions.

1 Do you support or oppose candidates in **political campaigns** in any way? If "Yes," explain. ☐ **Yes** ☐ **No**

2a Do you attempt to **influence legislation**? If "Yes," explain how you attempt to influence legislation and complete line 2b. If "No," go to line 3a. ☐ **Yes** ☐ **No**

b Have you made or are you making an **election** to have your legislative activities measured by expenditures by filing Form 5768? If "Yes," attach a copy of the Form 5768 that was already filed or attach a completed Form 5768 that you are filing with this application. If "No," describe whether your attempts to influence legislation are a substantial part of your activities. Include the time and money spent on your attempts to influence legislation as compared to your total activities. ☐ **Yes** ☐ **No**

3a Do you or will you operate bingo or **gaming** activities? If "Yes," describe who conducts them, and list all revenue received or expected to be received and expenses paid or expected to be paid in operating these activities. **Revenue and expenses** should be provided for the time periods specified in Part IX, Financial Data. ☐ **Yes** ☐ **No**

b Do you or will you enter into contracts or other agreements with individuals or organizations to conduct bingo or gaming for you? If "Yes," describe any written or oral arrangements that you made or intend to make, identify with whom you have or will have such arrangements, explain how the terms are or will be negotiated at arm's length, and explain how you determine or will determine you pay no more than fair market value or you will be paid at least fair market value. Attach copies or any written contracts or other agreements relating to such arrangements. ☐ **Yes** ☐ **No**

c List the states and local jurisdictions, including Indian Reservations, in which you conduct or will conduct gaming or bingo.

Part VIII   **Your Specific Activities** *(Continued)*

4a   Do you or will you undertake **fundraising**? If "Yes," check all the fundraising programs you do or will   ☐ **Yes**   ☐ **No**
conduct. See instructions.

☐ mail solicitations	☐ phone solicitations
☐ email solicitations	☐ accept donations on your website
☐ personal solicitations	☐ receive donations from another organization's website
☐ vehicle, boat, plane, or similar donations	☐ government grant solicitations
☐ foundation grant solicitations	☐ Other

Attach a description of each fundraising program.

b   Do you or will you have written or oral contracts with any individuals or organizations to raise funds for   ☐ **Yes**   ☐ **No**
you? If "Yes," describe these activities. Include all revenue and expenses from these activities and state
who conducts them. Revenue and expenses should be provided for the time periods specified in Part IX,
Financial Data. Also, attach a copy of any contracts or agreements.

c   Do you or will you engage in fundraising activities for other organizations? If "Yes," describe these   ☐ **Yes**   ☐ **No**
arrangements. Include a description of the organizations for which you raise funds and attach copies of
all contracts or agreements.

d   List all states and local jurisdictions in which you conduct fundraising. For each state or local jurisdiction
listed, specify whether you fundraise for your own organization, you fundraise for another organization, or
another organization fundraises for you.

e   Do you or will you maintain separate accounts for any contributor under which the contributor has the   ☐ **Yes**   ☐ **No**
right to advise on the use or distribution of funds? Answer "Yes" if the donor may provide advice on the
types of investments, distributions from the types of investments, or the distribution from the donor's
contribution account. If "Yes," describe this program, including the type of advice that may be provided
and submit copies of any written materials provided to donors.

5   Are you **affiliated** with a governmental unit? If "Yes," explain.   ☐ **Yes**   ☐ **No**

6a   Do you or will you engage in **economic development**? If "Yes," describe your program.   ☐ **Yes**   ☐ **No**
b   Describe in full who benefits from your economic development activities and how the activities promote
exempt purposes.

7a   Do or will persons other than your employees or volunteers **develop** your facilities? If "Yes," describe   ☐ **Yes**   ☐ **No**
each facility, the role of the developer, and any business or family relationship(s) between the developer
and your officers, directors, or trustees.

b   Do or will persons other than your employees or volunteers **manage** your activities or facilities? If "Yes,"   ☐ **Yes**   ☐ **No**
describe each activity and facility, the role of the manager, and any business or family relationship(s)
between the manager and your officers, directors, or trustees.

c   If there is a business or family relationship between any manager or developer and your officers,
directors, or trustees, identify the individuals, explain the relationship, describe how contracts are
negotiated at arm's length so that you pay no more than fair market value, and submit a copy of any
contracts or other agreements.

8   Do you or will you enter into **joint ventures**, including partnerships or **limited liability companies**   ☐ **Yes**   ☐ **No**
treated as partnerships, in which you share profits and losses with partners other than section 501(c)(3)
organizations? If "Yes," describe the activities of these joint ventures in which you participate.

9a   Are you applying for exemption as a childcare organization under section 501(k)? If "Yes," answer lines   ☐ **Yes**   ☐ **No**
9b through 9d. If "No," go to line 10.
b   Do you provide childcare so that parents or caretakers of children you care for can be **gainfully**   ☐ **Yes**   ☐ **No**
employed (see instructions)? If "No," explain how you qualify as a childcare organization described in
section 501(k).

c   Of the children for whom you provide childcare, are 85% or more of them cared for by you to enable their   ☐ **Yes**   ☐ **No**
parents or caretakers to be gainfully employed (see instructions)? If "No," explain how you qualify as a
childcare organization described in section 501(k).

d   Are your services available to the general public? If "No," describe the specific group of people for whom   ☐ **Yes**   ☐ **No**
your activities are available. Also, see the instructions and explain how you qualify as a childcare
organization described in section 501(k).

10   Do you or will you publish, own, or have rights in music, literature, tapes, artworks, choreography,   ☐ **Yes**   ☐ **No**
scientific discoveries, or other **intellectual property**? If "Yes," explain. Describe who owns or will own
any copyrights, patents, or trademarks, whether fees are or will be charged, how the fees are
determined, and how any items are or will be produced, distributed, and marketed.

Part VIII	Your Specific Activities *(Continued)*

11   Do you or will you accept contributions of: real property; conservation easements; closely held ☐ **Yes**   ☐ **No**
securities; intellectual property such as patents, trademarks, and copyrights; works of music or art;
licenses; royalties; automobiles, boats, planes, or other vehicles; or collectibles of any type? If "Yes,"
describe each type of contribution, any conditions imposed by the donor on the contribution, and any
agreements with the donor regarding the contribution.

12a   Do you or will you operate in a **foreign country** or **countries?** If "Yes," answer lines 12b through 12d. If ☐ **Yes**   ☐ **No**
"No," go to line 13a.

   b   Name the foreign countries and regions within the countries in which you operate.

   c   Describe your operations in each country and region in which you operate.

   d   Describe how your operations in each country and region further your exempt purposes.

13a   Do you or will you make grants, loans, or other distributions to organization(s)? If "Yes," answer lines 13b ☐ **Yes**   ☐ **No**
through 13g. If "No," go to line 14a.

   b   Describe how your grants, loans, or other distributions to organizations further your exempt purposes.

   c   Do you have written contracts with each of these organizations? If "Yes," attach a copy of each contract. ☐ **Yes**   ☐ **No**

   d   Identify each recipient organization and any **relationship** between you and the recipient organization.

   e   Describe the records you keep with respect to the grants, loans, or other distributions you make.

   f   Describe your selection process, including whether you do any of the following.

      (i)   Do you require an application form? If "Yes," attach a copy of the form. ☐ **Yes**   ☐ **No**

      (ii)   Do you require a grant proposal? If "Yes," describe whether the grant proposal specifies your ☐ **Yes**   ☐ **No**
responsibilities and those of the grantee, obligates the grantee to use the grant funds only for the
purposes for which the grant was made, provides for periodic written reports concerning the use of
grant funds, requires a final written report and an accounting of how grant funds were used, and
acknowledges your authority to withhold and/or recover grant funds in case such funds are, or appear
to be, misused.

   g   Describe your procedures for oversight of distributions that assure you the resources are used to further
your exempt purposes, including whether you require periodic and final reports on the use of resources.

14a   Do you or will you make grants, loans, or other distributions to foreign organizations? If "Yes," answer ☐ **Yes**   ☐ **No**
lines 14b through 14f. If "No," go to line 15.

   b   Provide the name of each foreign organization, the country and regions within a country in which each
foreign organization operates, and describe any relationship you have with each foreign organization.

   c   Does any foreign organization listed in line 14b accept contributions earmarked for a specific country or ☐ **Yes**   ☐ **No**
specific organization? If "Yes," list all earmarked organizations or countries.

   d   Do your contributors know that you have ultimate authority to use contributions made to you at your ☐ **Yes**   ☐ **No**
discretion for purposes consistent with your exempt purposes? If "Yes," describe how you relay this
information to contributors.

   e   Do you or will you make pre-grant inquiries about the recipient organization? If "Yes," describe these ☐ **Yes**   ☐ **No**
inquiries, including whether you inquire about the recipient's financial status, its tax-exempt status under
the Internal Revenue Code, its ability to accomplish the purpose for which the resources are provided,
and other relevant information.

   f   Do you or will you use any additional procedures to ensure that your distributions to foreign ☐ **Yes**   ☐ **No**
organizations are used in furtherance of your exempt purposes? If "Yes," describe these procedures,
including site visits by your employees or compliance checks by impartial experts, to verify that grant
funds are being used appropriately.

Part VIII	**Your Specific Activities** *(Continued)*		
15	Do you have a **close connection** with any organizations? If "Yes," explain.	☐ Yes	☐ No
16	Are you applying for exemption as a **cooperative hospital service organization** under section 501(e)? If "Yes," explain.	☐ Yes	☐ No
17	Are you applying for exemption as a **cooperative service organization of operating educational organizations** under section 501(f)? If "Yes," explain.	☐ Yes	☐ No
18	Are you applying for exemption as a **charitable risk pool** under section 501(n)? If "Yes," explain.	☐ Yes	☐ No
19	Do you or will you operate a **school**? If "Yes," complete Schedule B. Answer "Yes," whether you operate a school as your main function or as a secondary activity.	☐ Yes	☐ No
20	Is your main function to provide **hospital** or **medical care**? If "Yes," complete Schedule C.	☐ Yes	☐ No
21	Do you or will you provide **low-income housing** or housing for the **elderly** or **handicapped**? If "Yes," complete Schedule F.	☐ Yes	☐ No
22	Do you or will you provide scholarships, fellowships, educational loans, or other educational grants to individuals, including grants for travel, study, or other similar purposes? If "Yes," complete Schedule H. **Note: Private foundations** may use Schedule H to request advance approval of individual grant procedures.	☐ Yes	☐ No

Part IX	Financial Data

For purposes of this schedule, years in existence refer to completed tax years.

1. If in existence less than 5 years, complete the statement for each year in existence and provide projections of your likely revenues and expenses based on a reasonable and good faith estimate of your future finances for a total of:

   a. Three years of financial information if you have not completed one tax year, or

   b. Four years of financial information if you have completed one tax year. See instructions.

2. If in existence 5 or more years, complete the schedule for the most recent 5 tax years. You will need to provide a separate statement that includes information about the most recent 5 tax years because the data table in Part IX has not been updated to provide for a 5th year. See instructions.

A. Statement of Revenues and Expenses

	Type of revenue or expense	Current tax year	3 prior tax years or 2 succeeding tax years			(e) Provide Total for (a) through (d)
		(a) From _____ To _____	(b) From _____ To _____	(c) From _____ To _____	(d) From _____ To _____	
Revenues	1 Gifts, grants, and contributions received (do not include unusual grants)					
	2 Membership fees received					
	3 Gross investment income					
	4 Net unrelated business income					
	5 Taxes levied for your benefit					
	6 Value of services or facilities furnished by a governmental unit without charge (not including the value of services generally furnished to the public without charge)					
	7 Any revenue not otherwise listed above or in lines 9–12 below (attach an itemized list)					
	8 Total of lines 1 through 7					
	9 Gross receipts from admissions, merchandise sold or services performed, or furnishing of facilities in any activity that is related to your exempt purposes (attach itemized list)					
	10 Total of lines 8 and 9					
	11 Net gain or loss on sale of capital assets (attach schedule and see instructions)					
	12 **Unusual grants**					
	13 Total Revenue Add lines 10 through 12					
Expenses	14 Fundraising expenses					
	15 Contributions, gifts, grants, and similar amounts paid out (attach an itemized list)					
	16 Disbursements to or for the benefit of members (attach an itemized list)					
	17 Compensation of officers, directors, and trustees					
	18 Other salaries and wages					
	19 Interest expense					
	20 Occupancy (rent, utilities, etc.)					
	21 Depreciation and depletion					
	22 Professional fees					
	23 Any expense not otherwise classified, such as program services (attach itemized list)					
	24 Total Expenses Add lines 14 through 23					

Form **1023** (Rev. 12-2017)

Part IX	Financial Data *(Continued)*

B. Balance Sheet (for your most recently completed tax year)

	Assets		Year End: (Whole dollars)
1	Cash	1	
2	Accounts receivable, net	2	
3	Inventories	3	
4	Bonds and notes receivable (attach an itemized list)	4	
5	Corporate stocks (attach an itemized list)	5	
6	Loans receivable (attach an itemized list)	6	
7	Other investments (attach an itemized list)	7	
8	Depreciable and depletable assets (attach an itemized list)	8	
9	Land	9	
10	Other assets (attach an itemized list)	10	
11	Total Assets (add lines 1 through 10)	11	
	Liabilities		
12	Accounts payable	12	
13	Contributions, gifts, grants, etc. payable	13	
14	Mortgages and notes payable (attach an itemized list)	14	
15	Other liabilities (attach an itemized list)	15	
16	Total Liabilities (add lines 12 through 15)	16	
	Fund Balances or Net Assets		
17	Total fund balances or net assets	17	
18	Total Liabilities and Fund Balances or Net Assets (add lines 16 and 17)	18	
19	Have there been any substantial changes in your assets or liabilities since the end of the period shown above? If "Yes," explain.	☐ Yes ☐ No	

Part X	Public Charity Status

Part X is designed to classify you as an organization that is either a **private foundation** or a **public charity**. Public charity status is a more favorable tax status than private foundation status. If you are a private foundation, Part X is designed to further determine whether you are a **private operating foundation**. See instructions.

1a Are you a private foundation? If "Yes," go to line 1b. If "No," go to line 5 and proceed as instructed. If you are unsure, see the instructions. ☐ Yes ☐ No

b As a private foundation, section 508(e) requires special provisions in your organizing document in addition to those that apply to all organizations described in section 501(c)(3). Check the box to confirm that your organizing document meets this requirement, whether by express provision or by reliance on operation of state law. Attach a statement that describes specifically where your organizing document meets this requirement, such as a reference to a particular article or section in your organizing document or by operation of state law. See the instructions, including Appendix B, for information about the special provisions that need to be contained in your organizing document. Go to line 2. ☐

2 Are you a private operating foundation? To be a private operating foundation you must engage directly in the active conduct of charitable, religious, educational, and similar activities, as opposed to indirectly carrying out these activities by providing grants to individuals or other organizations. If "Yes," go to line 3. If "No," go to the signature section of Part XI. ☐ Yes ☐ No

3 Have you existed for one or more years? If "Yes," attach financial information showing that you are a private operating foundation; go to the signature section of Part XI. If "No," continue to line 4. ☐ Yes ☐ No

4 Have you attached either (1) an affidavit or opinion of counsel, (including a written affidavit or opinion from a certified public accountant or accounting firm with expertise regarding this tax law matter), that sets forth facts concerning your operations and support to demonstrate that you are likely to satisfy the requirements to be classified as a private operating foundation; or (2) a statement describing your proposed operations as a private operating foundation? ☐ Yes ☐ No

5 If you answered "No" to line 1a, indicate the type of public charity status you are requesting by checking one of the choices below. You may check only one box.

The organization is not a private foundation because it is:

a 509(a)(1) and 170(b)(1)(A)(i)—a church or a convention or association of churches. Complete and attach Schedule A. ☐

b 509(a)(1) and 170(b)(1)(A)(ii)—a **school**. Complete and attach Schedule B. ☐

c 509(a)(1) and 170(b)(1)(A)(iii)—a **hospital**, a cooperative hospital service organization, or a medical research organization operated in conjunction with a hospital. Complete and attach Schedule C. ☐

d 509(a)(3)—an organization supporting either one or more organizations described in line 5a through c, f, h, or i or a publicly supported section 501(c)(4), (5), or (6) organization. Complete and attach Schedule D. ☐

Part X   **Public Charity Status** *(Continued)*

e	509(a)(4) – an organization organized and operated exclusively for testing for public safety.	☐
f	509(a)(1) and 170(b)(1)(A)(iv) – an organization operated for the benefit of a college or university that is owned or operated by a governmental unit.	☐
g	509(a)(1) and 170(b)(1)(A)(ix) – an agricultural research organization directly engaged in the continuous active conduct of agricultural research in conjunction with a college or university.	☐
h	509(a)(1) and 170(b)(1)(A)(vi) – an organization that receives a substantial part of its financial support in the form of contributions from publicly supported organizations, from a governmental unit, or from the general public.	☐
i	509(a)(2) – an organization that normally receives not more than one-third of its financial support from gross **investment income** and receives more than one-third of its financial support from contributions, membership fees, and gross receipts from activities related to its exempt functions (subject to certain exceptions).	☐
j	A publicly supported organization, but unsure if it is described in 5h or 5i. You would like the IRS to decide the correct status.	☐

6   If you checked box h, i, or j in question 5 above, and you have been in existence more than 5 years, you must confirm your public support status. Answer line 6a if you checked box h in line 5 above. Answer line 6b if you checked box i in line 5 above. If you checked box j in line 5 above, answer both lines 6a and 6b.

a   (i)   Enter 2% of line 8, column (e) on Part IX-A Statement of Revenues and Expenses   _____

      (ii) Attach a list showing the name and amount contributed by each person, company, or organization whose gifts totaled more than the 2% amount. If the answer is "None," state this.

b   (i)   For each year amounts are included on lines 1, 2, and 9 of Part IX-A Statement of Revenues and Expenses, attach a list showing the name and amount received from each **disqualified person.** If the answer is "None," state this.

      (ii) For each year amounts were included on line 9 of Part IX-A Statement of Revenues and Expenses, attach a list showing the name of and amount received from each payer, other than a disqualified person, whose payments were more than the larger of (1) 1% of Line 10, Part IX-A Statement of Revenues and Expenses, or (2) $5,000. If the answer is "None," state this.

7   Did you receive any unusual grants during any of the years shown on Part IX-A Statement of Revenues and Expenses? If "Yes," attach a list including the name of the contributor, the date and amount of the grant, a brief description of the grant, and explain why it is unusual.   ☐ **Yes**   ☐ **No**

Part XI   **User Fee Information and Signature**

You must include the correct user fee payment with this application. If you do not submit the correct user fee, we will not process the application and we will return it to you. Your check or money order must be made payable to the United States Treasury. User fees are subject to change. Check our website at *www.irs.gov* and type "Exempt Organizations User Fee" in the search box, or call Customer Account Services at 1-877-829-5500 for current information.

                  Enter the amount of the user fee paid: _____

I declare under the penalties of perjury that I am authorized to sign this application on behalf of the above organization and that I have examined this application, including the accompanying schedules and attachments, and to the best of my knowledge it is true, correct, and complete.

Please
Sign ▶
Here

_____ (Signature of Officer, Director, Trustee, or other authorized official)	_____ (Type or print name of signer)	_____ (Date)
	_____ (Type or print title or authority of signer)	

[This page left blank intentionally]

Schedule A. Churches

1a	Do you have a written creed, statement of faith, or summary of beliefs? If "Yes," attach copies of relevant documents.	☐ Yes	☐ No
b	Do you have a form of worship? If "Yes," describe your form of worship.	☐ Yes	☐ No
2a	Do you have a formal code of doctrine and discipline? If "Yes," describe your code of doctrine and discipline.	☐ Yes	☐ No
b	Do you have a distinct religious history? If "Yes," describe your religious history.	☐ Yes	☐ No
c	Do you have a literature of your own? If "Yes," describe your literature.	☐ Yes	☐ No
3	Describe the organization's religious hierarchy or ecclesiastical government.		
4a	Do you have regularly scheduled religious services? If "Yes," describe the nature of the services and provide representative copies of relevant literature such as church bulletins.	☐ Yes	☐ No
b	What is the average attendance at your regularly scheduled religious services?		
5a	Do you have an established place of worship? If "Yes," refer to the instructions for the information required.	☐ Yes	☐ No
b	Do you own the property where you have an established place of worship?	☐ Yes	☐ No
6	Do you have an established congregation or other regular membership group? If "No," refer to the instructions.	☐ Yes	☐ No
7	How many members do you have?		
8a	Do you have a process by which an individual becomes a member? If "Yes," describe the process and complete lines 8b–8d, below.	☐ Yes	☐ No
b	If you have members, do your members have voting rights, rights to participate in religious functions, or other rights? If "Yes," describe the rights your members have.	☐ Yes	☐ No
c	May your members be associated with another denomination or church?	☐ Yes	☐ No
d	Are all of your members part of the same **family**?	☐ Yes	☐ No
9	Do you conduct baptisms, weddings, funerals, etc.?	☐ Yes	☐ No
10	Do you have a school for the religious instruction of the young?	☐ Yes	☐ No
11a	Do you have a minister or religious leader? If "Yes," describe this person's role and explain whether the minister or religious leader was ordained, commissioned, or licensed after a prescribed course of study.	☐ Yes	☐ No
b	Do you have schools for the preparation of your ordained ministers or religious leaders?	☐ Yes	☐ No
12	Is your minister or religious leader also one of your officers, directors, or trustees?	☐ Yes	☐ No
13	Do you ordain, commission, or license ministers or religious leaders? If "Yes," describe the requirements for ordination, commission, or licensure.	☐ Yes	☐ No
14	Are you part of a group of churches with similar beliefs and structures? If "Yes," explain. Include the name of the group of churches.	☐ Yes	☐ No
15	Do you issue church charters? If "Yes," describe the requirements for issuing a charter.	☐ Yes	☐ No
16	Did you pay a fee for a church charter? If "Yes," attach a copy of the charter.	☐ Yes	☐ No
17	Do you have other information you believe should be considered regarding your status as a church? If "Yes," explain.	☐ Yes	☐ No

Form **1023** (Rev. 12-2017)

Schedule B. Schools, Colleges, and Universities

If you operate a school as an activity, complete Schedule B

Section I   Operational Information

1a	Do you normally have a regularly scheduled curriculum, a regular faculty of qualified teachers, a regularly enrolled student body, and facilities where your educational activities are regularly carried on? If "No," do not complete the remainder of Schedule B.	☐ Yes ☐ No
b	Is the primary function of your school the presentation of formal instruction? If "Yes," describe your school in terms of whether it is an elementary, secondary, college, technical, or other type of school. If "No," do not complete the remainder of Schedule B.	☐ Yes ☐ No
2a	Are you a public school because you are operated by a state or subdivision of a state? If "Yes," explain how you are operated by a state or subdivision of a state. Do not complete the remainder of Schedule B.	☐ Yes ☐ No
b	Are you a public school because you are operated wholly or predominantly from government funds or property? If "Yes," explain how you are operated wholly or predominantly from government funds or property. Submit a copy of your funding agreement regarding government funding. Do not complete the remainder of Schedule B.	☐ Yes ☐ No
3	In what public school district, county, and state are you located?	
4	Were you formed or substantially expanded at the time of public school desegregation in the above school district or county?	☐ Yes ☐ No
5	Has a state or federal administrative agency or judicial body ever determined that you are racially discriminatory? If "Yes," explain.	☐ Yes ☐ No
6	Has your right to receive financial aid or assistance from a governmental agency ever been revoked or suspended? If "Yes," explain.	☐ Yes ☐ No
7	Do you or will you contract with another organization to develop, build, market, or finance your facilities? If "Yes," explain how that entity is selected, explain how the terms of any contracts or other agreements are negotiated at arm's length, and explain how you determine that you will pay no more than fair market value for services. **Note:** Make sure your answer is consistent with the information provided in Part VIII, line 7a.	☐ Yes ☐ No
8	Do you or will you manage your activities or facilities through your own employees or volunteers? If "No," attach a statement describing the activities that will be managed by others, the names of the persons or organizations that manage or will manage your activities or facilities, and how these managers were or will be selected. Also, submit copies of any contracts, proposed contracts, or other agreements regarding the provision of management services for your activities or facilities. Explain how the terms of any contracts or other agreements were or will be negotiated, and explain how you determine you will pay no more than fair market value for services. **Note:** Answer "Yes" if you manage or intend to manage your programs through your own employees or by using volunteers. Answer "No" if you engage or intend to engage a separate organization or independent contractor. Make sure your answer is consistent with the information provided in Part VIII, line 7b.	☐ Yes ☐ No

Section II   Establishment of Racially Nondiscriminatory Policy

Information required by **Revenue Procedure 75-50.**

1	Have you adopted a racially nondiscriminatory policy as to students in your organizing document, bylaws, or by resolution of your governing body? If "Yes," state where the policy can be found or supply a copy of the policy. If "No," you must adopt a nondiscriminatory policy as to students before submitting this application. See Pub. 557.	☐ Yes ☐ No
2	Do your brochures, application forms, advertisements, and catalogues dealing with student admissions, programs, and scholarships contain a statement of your racially nondiscriminatory policy?	☐ Yes ☐ No
a	If "Yes," attach a representative sample of each document.	
b	If "No," by checking the box to the right you agree that all future printed materials, including website content, will contain the required nondiscriminatory policy statement.	▶ ☐
3	Have you published a notice of your nondiscriminatory policy in a newspaper of general circulation that serves all racial segments of the community? See the instructions for specific requirements. If "No," explain.	☐ Yes ☐ No
4	Does or will the organization (or any department or division within it) discriminate in any way on the basis of race with respect to admissions; use of facilities or exercise of student privileges; faculty or administrative staff; or scholarship or loan programs? If "Yes," for any of the above, explain fully.	☐ Yes ☐ No

Form **1023** (Rev. 12-2017)

Schedule B. Schools, Colleges, and Universities *(Continued)*

5   Complete the table below to show the racial composition for the current academic year and projected for the next academic year, of: (a) the student body, (b) the faculty, and (c) the administrative staff. Provide actual numbers rather than percentages for each racial category.

If you are not operational, submit an estimate based on the best information available (such as the racial composition of the community served).

Racial Category	(a) Student Body		(b) Faculty		(c) Administrative Staff	
	Current Year	Next Year	Current Year	Next Year	Current Year	Next Year
Total						

6   In the table below, provide the number and amount of loans and scholarships awarded to students enrolled by racial categories.

Racial Category	Number of Loans		Amount of Loans		Number of Scholarships		Amount of Scholarships	
	Current Year	Next Year	Current Year	Next Year	Current Year	Next Year	Current Year	Next Year
Total								

7a   Attach a list of your incorporators, founders, board members, and donors of land or buildings, whether individuals or organizations.

  b   Do any of these individuals or organizations have an objective to maintain segregated public or private   ☐ **Yes**   ☐ **No**
      school education? If "Yes," explain.

8   Will you maintain records according to the nondiscrimination provisions contained in Revenue Procedure   ☐ **Yes**   ☐ **No**
    75-50? If "No," explain. See instructions.

Schedule C. Hospitals and Medical Research Organizations

Check the box if you are a **hospital**. See the instructions for a definition of the term "hospital," which includes an organization whose principal purpose or function is providing **hospital** or **medical care**. Complete Section I below. ☐

Check the box if you are a **medical research organization** operated in conjunction with a hospital. See the instructions for a definition of the term "medical research organization," which refers to an organization whose principal purpose or function is medical research and which is directly engaged in the continuous active conduct of medical research in conjunction with a hospital. Complete Section II. ☐

Section I   Hospitals

1a	Are all the doctors in the community eligible for staff privileges? If "No," give the reasons why and explain how the medical staff is selected.	☐ Yes	☐ No
2a	Do you or will you provide medical services to all individuals in your community who can pay for themselves or have private health insurance? If "No," explain.	☐ Yes	☐ No
b	Do you or will you provide medical services to all individuals in your community who participate in Medicare? If "No," explain.	☐ Yes	☐ No
c	Do you or will you provide medical services to all individuals in your community who participate in Medicaid? If "No," explain.	☐ Yes	☐ No
3a	Do you or will you require persons covered by Medicare or Medicaid to pay a deposit before receiving services? If "Yes," explain.	☐ Yes	☐ No
b	Does the same deposit requirement, if any, apply to all other patients? If "No," explain.	☐ Yes	☐ No
4a	Do you or will you maintain a full-time emergency room? If "No," explain why you do not maintain a full-time emergency room. Also, describe any emergency services that you provide.	☐ Yes	☐ No
b	Do you have a policy on providing emergency services to persons without apparent means to pay? If "Yes," provide a copy of the policy.	☐ Yes	☐ No
c	Do you have any arrangements with police, fire, and voluntary ambulance services for the delivery or admission of emergency cases? If "Yes," describe the arrangements, including whether they are written or oral agreements. If written, submit copies of all such agreements.	☐ Yes	☐ No
5a	Do you provide for a portion of your services and facilities to be used for charity patients? If "Yes," answer 5b through 5e.	☐ Yes	☐ No
b	Explain your policy regarding charity cases, including how you distinguish between charity care and bad debts. Submit a copy of your written policy.		
c	Provide data on your past experience in admitting charity patients, including amounts you expend for treating charity care patients and types of services you provide to charity care patients.		
d	Describe any arrangements you have with federal, state, or local governments or government agencies for paying for the cost of treating charity care patients. Submit copies of any written agreements.		
e	Do you provide services on a sliding fee schedule depending on financial ability to pay? If "Yes," submit your sliding fee schedule.	☐ Yes	☐ No
6a	Do you or will you carry on a formal program of medical training or medical research? If "Yes," describe such programs, including the type of programs offered, the scope of such programs, and affiliations with other hospitals or medical care providers with which you carry on the medical training or research programs.	☐ Yes	☐ No
b	Do you or will you carry on a formal program of community education? If "Yes," describe such programs, including the type of programs offered, the scope of such programs, and affiliation with other hospitals or medical care providers with which you offer community education programs.	☐ Yes	☐ No
7	Do you or will you provide office space to physicians carrying on their own medical practices? If "Yes," describe the criteria for who may use the space, explain the means used to determine that you are paid at least fair market value, and submit representative lease agreements.	☐ Yes	☐ No
8	Is your board of directors comprised of a majority of individuals who are representative of the community you serve? Include a list of each board member's name and business, financial, or professional relationship with the hospital. Also, identify each board member who is representative of the community and describe how that individual is a community representative.	☐ Yes	☐ No
9	Do you participate in any joint ventures? If "Yes," state your ownership percentage in each joint venture, list your investment in each joint venture, describe the tax status of other participants in each joint venture (including whether they are section 501(c)(3) organizations), describe the activities of each joint venture, describe how you exercise control over the activities of each joint venture, and describe how each joint venture furthers your exempt purposes. Also, submit copies of all agreements.	☐ Yes	☐ No

Note: Make sure your answer is consistent with the information provided in Part VIII, line 8.

Form **1023** (Rev. 12-2017)

47

Schedule C. Hospitals and Medical Research Organizations *(Continued)*

Section I   **Hospitals** *(Continued)*

10	Do you or will you manage your activities or facilities through your own employees or volunteers? If "No," attach a statement describing the activities that will be managed by others, the names of the persons or organizations that manage or will manage your activities or facilities, and how these managers were or will be selected. Also, submit copies of any contracts, proposed contracts, or other agreements regarding the provision of management services for your activities or facilities. Explain how the terms of any contracts or other agreements were or will be negotiated, and explain how you determine you will pay no more than fair market value for services. **Note:** Answer "Yes" if you do manage or intend to manage your programs through your own employees or by using volunteers. Answer "No" if you engage or intend to engage a separate organization or independent contractor. Make sure your answer is consistent with the information provided in Part VIII, line 7b.	☐ Yes	☐ No
11	Do you or will you offer recruitment incentives to physicians? If "Yes," describe your recruitment incentives and attach copies of all written recruitment incentive policies.	☐ Yes	☐ No
12	Do you or will you lease equipment, assets, or office space from physicians who have a financial or professional relationship with you? If "Yes," explain how you establish a fair market value for the lease.	☐ Yes	☐ No
13	Have you purchased medical practices, ambulatory surgery centers, or other business assets from physicians or other persons with whom you have a business relationship, aside from the purchase? If "Yes," submit a copy of each purchase and sales contract and describe how you arrived at fair market value, including copies of appraisals.	☐ Yes	☐ No
14	Have you adopted a **conflict of interest policy** consistent with the sample health care organization conflict of interest policy in Appendix A of the instructions? If "Yes," submit a copy of the policy and explain how the policy has been adopted, such as by resolution of your governing board. If "No," explain how you will avoid any conflicts of interest in your business dealings.	☐ Yes	☐ No

Section II   **Medical Research Organizations**

1	Name the hospitals with which you have a relationship and describe the relationship. Attach copies of written agreements with each hospital that demonstrate continuing relationships between you and the hospital(s).
2	Attach a schedule describing your present and proposed activities for the direct conduct of medical research; describe the nature of the activities, and the amount of money that has been or will be spent in carrying them out.
3	Attach a schedule of assets showing their fair market value and the portion of your assets directly devoted to medical research.

Form **1023** (Rev. 12-2017)

Schedule D. Section 509(a)(3) Supporting Organizations

Section I　　Identifying Information About the Supported Organization(s)

1　State the names, addresses, and EINs of the supported organizations. If additional space is needed, attach a separate sheet.

Name	Address	EIN

2　Are all supported organizations listed in line 1 public charities under section 509(a)(1) or (2)? If "Yes," go to Section II. If "No," go to line 3. ☐ Yes　☐ No

3　Do the supported organizations have tax-exempt status under section 501(c)(4), 501(c)(5), or 501(c)(6)? ☐ Yes　☐ No
　　If "Yes," for each 501(c)(4), (5), or (6) organization supported, provide the following financial information.
　　• Part IX-A. Statement of Revenues and Expenses, lines 1–13, and
　　• Part X, lines 6b(i), 6b(ii), and 7.
　　If "No," attach a statement describing how each organization you support is a public charity under section 509(a)(1) or (2).

Section II　　Relationship with Supported Organization(s)—Three Tests

To be classified as a supporting organization, an organization must meet one of three relationship tests.
　　Test 1: "Operated, supervised, or controlled by" one or more publicly supported organizations, or
　　Test 2: "Supervised or controlled in connection with" one or more publicly supported organizations, or
　　Test 3: "Operated in connection with" one or more publicly supported organizations.

1　Information to establish the "operated, supervised, or controlled by" relationship (Test 1)
　　Is a majority of your governing board or officers elected or appointed by the supported organization(s)? ☐ Yes　☐ No
　　If "Yes," describe the process by which your governing board is appointed and elected; go to Section III.
　　If "No," continue to line 2.

2　Information to establish the "supervised or controlled in connection with" relationship (Test 2)
　　Does a majority of your governing board consist of individuals who also serve on the governing board of ☐ Yes　☐ No
　　the supported organization(s)? If "Yes," describe the process by which your governing board is appointed
　　and elected; go to Section III. If "No," go to line 3.

3　Information to establish the "operated in connection with" responsiveness test (Test 3)
　　Are you a trust from which the named supported organization(s) can enforce and compel an accounting ☐ Yes　☐ No
　　under state law? If "Yes," explain whether you advised the supported organization(s) in writing of these
　　rights and provide a copy of the written communication documenting this; go to Section II, line 5. If "No,"
　　go to line 4a.

4　Information to establish the alternative "operated in connection with" responsiveness test (Test 3)

a　Do the officers, directors, trustees, or members of the supported organization(s) elect or appoint one or ☐ Yes　☐ No
　　more of your officers, directors, or trustees? If "Yes," explain and provide documentation; go to line 4d,
　　below. If "No," go to line 4b.

b　Do one or more members of the governing body of the supported organization(s) also serve as your ☐ Yes　☐ No
　　officers, directors, or trustees or hold other important offices with respect to you? If "Yes," explain and
　　provide documentation; go to line 4d, below. If "No," go to line 4c.

c　Do your officers, directors, or trustees maintain a close and continuous working relationship with the ☐ Yes　☐ No
　　officers, directors, or trustees of the supported organization(s)? If "Yes," explain and provide
　　documentation.

d　Do the supported organization(s) have a significant voice in your investment policies, in the making and ☐ Yes　☐ No
　　timing of grants, and in otherwise directing the use of your income or assets? If "Yes," explain and
　　provide documentation.

e　Describe and provide copies of written communications documenting how you made the supported
　　organization(s) aware of your supporting activities.

5　Information to establish the "operated in connection with" integral part test (Test 3)
　　Do you conduct activities that would otherwise be carried out by the supported organization(s)? If "Yes," ☐ Yes　☐ No
　　explain and go to Section III. If "No," continue to line 6a.

Schedule D. Section 509(a)(3) Supporting Organizations *(Continued)*

Section II   Relationship with Supported Organization(s)—Three Tests *(Continued)*

6   Information to establish the alternative "operated in connection with" integral part test (Test 3)

a   Do you distribute at least 85% of your annual **net income** to the supported organization(s)? If "Yes," go to line 6b. See instructions.   ☐ **Yes**   ☐ **No**

If "No," state the percentage of your income that you distribute to each supported organization. Also explain how you ensure that the supported organization(s) are attentive to your operations.

b   How much do you contribute annually to each supported organization? Attach a schedule.

c   What is the total annual revenue of each supported organization? If you need additional space, attach a list.

d   Do you or the supported organization(s) **earmark** your funds for support of a particular program or activity? If "Yes," explain.   ☐ **Yes**   ☐ **No**

7a   Does your organizing document specify the supported organization(s) by name? If "Yes," state the article and paragraph number and go to Section III. If "No," answer line 7b.   ☐ **Yes**   ☐ **No**

b   Attach a statement describing whether there has been an historic and continuing relationship between you and the supported organization(s).

Section III   Organizational Test

1a   If you met relationship Test 1 or Test 2 in Section II, your organizing document must specify the supported organization(s) by name, or by naming a similar purpose or charitable class of beneficiaries. If your organizing document complies with this requirement, answer "Yes." If your organizing document does not comply with this requirement, answer "No," and see the instructions.   ☐ **Yes**   ☐ **No**

b   If you met relationship Test 3 in Section II, your organizing document must generally specify the supported organization(s) by name. If your organizing document complies with this requirement, answer "Yes," and go to Section IV. If your organizing document does not comply with this requirement, answer "No," and see the instructions.   ☐ **Yes**   ☐ **No**

Section IV   Disqualified Person Test

You do not qualify as a supporting organization if you are **controlled** directly or indirectly by one or more **disqualified persons** (as defined in section 4946) other than **foundation managers** or one or more organizations that you support. Foundation managers who are also disqualified persons for another reason are disqualified persons with respect to you.

1a   Do any persons who are disqualified persons with respect to you, (except individuals who are disqualified persons only because they are foundation managers), appoint any of your foundation managers? If "Yes," (1) describe the process by which disqualified persons appoint any of your foundation managers, (2) provide the names of these disqualified persons and the foundation managers they appoint, and (3) explain how control is vested over your operations (including assets and activities) by persons other than disqualified persons.   ☐ **Yes**   ☐ **No**

b   Do any persons who have a family or business relationship with any disqualified persons with respect to you, (except individuals who are disqualified persons only because they are foundation managers), appoint any of your foundation managers? If "Yes," (1) describe the process by which individuals with a family or business relationship with disqualified persons appoint any of your foundation managers, (2) provide the names of these disqualified persons, the individuals with a family or business relationship with disqualified persons, and the foundation managers appointed, and (3) explain how control is vested over your operations (including assets and activities) in individuals other than disqualified persons.   ☐ **Yes**   ☐ **No**

c   Do any persons who are disqualified persons, (except individuals who are disqualified persons only because they are foundation managers), have any influence regarding your operations, including your assets or activities? If "Yes," (1) provide the names of these disqualified persons, (2) explain how influence is exerted over your operations (including assets and activities), and (3) explain how control is vested over your operations (including assets and activities) by individuals other than disqualified persons.   ☐ **Yes**   ☐ **No**

Schedule E. Organizations Not Filing Form 1023 Within 27 Months of Formation

Schedule E is intended to determine whether you are eligible for tax exemption under section 501(c)(3) from the postmark date of your application or from your date of incorporation or formation, whichever is earlier.

1	Are you a church, association of churches, or integrated auxiliary of a church? If "Yes," complete Schedule A and stop here. Do not complete the remainder of Schedule E.	☐ **Yes**	☐ **No**
2a	Are you a public charity with annual **gross receipts** that are normally $5,000 or less? If "Yes," stop here. Answer "No" if you are a private foundation, regardless of your gross receipts.	☐ **Yes**	☐ **No**
b	If your gross receipts were normally more than $5,000, are you filing this application within 90 days from the end of the tax year in which your gross receipts were normally more than $5,000? If "Yes," stop here.	☐ **Yes**	☐ **No**
3a	Were you included as a subordinate in a group exemption application or letter? If "No," go to line 4.	☐ **Yes**	☐ **No**
b	If you were included as a subordinate in a group exemption letter, are you filing this application within 27 months from the date you were notified by the organization holding the group exemption letter or the Internal Revenue Service that you cease to be covered by the group exemption letter? If "Yes," stop here.	☐ **Yes**	☐ **No**
c	If you were included as a subordinate in a timely filed group exemption request that was denied, are you filing this application within 27 months from the postmark date of the Internal Revenue Service final adverse ruling letter? If "Yes," stop here.	☐ **Yes**	☐ **No**
4	Were you created on or before October 9, 1969? If "Yes," stop here. Do not complete the remainder of this schedule.	☐ **Yes**	☐ **No**
5	If you answered "No" to lines 1 through 4, we cannot recognize you as tax exempt from your date of formation unless you qualify for an extension of time to apply for exemption. Do you wish to request an extension of time to apply to be recognized as exempt from the date you were formed? If "Yes," attach a statement explaining why you did not file this application within the 27-month period. Do not answer lines 6 or 7. If "No," go to line 6a.	☐ **Yes**	☐ **No**
6a	If you answered "No" to line 5, you can only be exempt under section 501(c)(3) from the postmark date of this application. Therefore, do you want us to treat this application as a request for tax exemption from the postmark date? **Note:** Be sure your ruling eligibility agrees with your answer to Part X, line 6.	☐ **Yes**	☐ **No**
b	Do you anticipate significant changes in your sources of support in the future? If "Yes," complete line 7 below.	☐ **Yes**	☐ **No**

Schedule E. Organizations Not Filing Form 1023 Within 27 Months of Formation *(Continued)*

7   Complete this item only if you answered "Yes" to line 6b. Include projected revenue for the first two full years following the current tax year.

Type of Revenue	Projected revenue for 2 years following current tax year		
	(a) From _____ To	(b) From _____ To	(c) Total
1 Gifts, grants, and contributions received (do not include unusual grants)			
2 Membership fees received			
3 Gross investment income			
4 Net unrelated business income			
5 Taxes levied for your benefit			
6 Value of services or facilities furnished by a governmental unit without charge (not including the value of services generally furnished to the public without charge)			
7 Any revenue not otherwise listed above or in lines 9–12 below (attach an itemized list)			
8 Total of lines 1 through 7			
9 Gross receipts from admissions, merchandise sold, or services performed, or furnishing of facilities in any activity that is related to your exempt purposes (attach itemized list)			
10 Total of lines 8 and 9			
11 Net gain or loss on sale of capital assets (attach an itemized list)			
12 Unusual grants			
13 Total revenue. Add lines 10 through 12			

Form **1023** (Rev. 12-2017)

Schedule F. Homes for the Elderly or Handicapped and Low-Income Housing

Section I	General Information About Your Housing

1   Describe the type of housing you provide.

2   Provide copies of any application forms you use for admission.

3   Explain how the public is made aware of your facility.

4a Provide a description of each facility.
  b What is the total number of residents each facility can accommodate?
  c What is your current number of residents in each facility?
  d Describe each facility in terms of whether residents rent or purchase housing from you.

5   Attach a sample copy of your residency or homeownership contract or agreement.

6   Do you participate in any joint ventures? If "Yes," state your ownership percentage in each joint venture, list your investment in each joint venture, describe the tax status of other participants in each joint venture (including whether they are section 501(c)(3) organizations), describe the activities of each joint venture, describe how you exercise control over the activities of each joint venture, and describe how each joint venture furthers your exempt purposes. Also, submit copies of all joint venture agreements. ☐ Yes ☐ No

    Note: Make sure your answer is consistent with the information provided in Part VIII, line 8.

7   Do you or will you contract with another organization to develop, build, market, or finance your housing? If "Yes," explain how that entity is selected, explain how the terms of any contract(s) are negotiated at arm's length, and explain how you determine you will pay no more than fair market value for services. ☐ Yes ☐ No

    Note: Make sure your answer is consistent with the information provided in Part VIII, line 7a.

8   Do you or will you manage your activities or facilities through your own employees or volunteers? If "No," attach a statement describing the activities that will be managed by others, the names of the persons or organizations that manage or will manage your activities or facilities, and how these managers were or will be selected. Also, submit copies of any contracts, proposed contracts, or other agreements regarding the provision of management services for your activities or facilities. Explain how the terms of any contracts or other agreements were or will be negotiated, and explain how you determine you will pay no more than fair market value for services. ☐ Yes ☐ No

    Note: Answer "Yes" if you do manage or intend to manage your programs through your own employees or by using volunteers. Answer "No" if you engage or intend to engage a separate organization or independent contractor. Make sure your answer is consistent with the information provided in Part VIII, line 7b.

9   Do you participate in any government housing programs? If "Yes," describe these programs. ☐ Yes ☐ No

10a Do you own the facility? If "No," describe any enforceable rights you possess to purchase the facility in the future; go to line 10c. If "Yes," answer line 10b. ☐ Yes ☐ No

  b How did you acquire the facility? For example, did you develop it yourself, purchase a project, etc. Attach all contracts, transfer agreements, or other documents connected with the acquisition of the facility.

  c Do you lease the facility or the land on which it is located? If "Yes," describe the parties to the lease(s) and provide copies of all leases. ☐ Yes ☐ No

Schedule F. Homes for the Elderly or Handicapped and Low-Income Housing *(Continued)*

Section II	**Homes for the Elderly or Handicapped**		
1a	Do you provide housing for the elderly? If "Yes," describe who qualifies for your housing in terms of age, infirmity, or other criteria and explain how you select persons for your housing.	☐ **Yes**	☐ **No**
b	Do you provide housing for the handicapped? If "Yes," describe who qualifies for your housing in terms of disability, income levels, or other criteria and explain how you select persons for your housing.	☐ **Yes**	☐ **No**
2a	Do you charge an entrance or founder's fee? If "Yes," describe what this charge covers, whether it is a one-time fee, how the fee is determined, whether it is payable in a lump sum or on an installment basis, whether it is refundable, and the circumstances, if any, under which it may be waived.	☐ **Yes**	☐ **No**
b	Do you charge periodic fees or maintenance charges? If "Yes," describe what these charges cover and how they are determined.	☐ **Yes**	☐ **No**
c	Is your housing affordable to a significant segment of the elderly or handicapped persons in the community? Identify your **community**. Also, if "Yes," explain how you determine your housing is affordable.	☐ **Yes**	☐ **No**
3a	Do you have an established policy concerning residents who become unable to pay their regular charges? If "Yes," describe your established policy.	☐ **Yes**	☐ **No**
b	Do you have any arrangements with government welfare agencies or others to absorb all or part of the cost of maintaining residents who become unable to pay their regular charges? If "Yes," describe these arrangements.	☐ **Yes**	☐ **No**
4	Do you have arrangements for the healthcare needs of your residents? If "Yes," describe these arrangements.	☐ **Yes**	☐ **No**
5	Are your facilities designed to meet the physical, emotional, recreational, social, religious, and/or other similar needs of the elderly or handicapped? If "Yes," describe these design features.	☐ **Yes**	☐ **No**

Section III	**Low-Income Housing**		
1	Do you provide low-income housing? If "Yes," describe who qualifies for your housing in terms of income levels or other criteria, and describe how you select persons for your housing.	☐ **Yes**	☐ **No**
2	In addition to rent or mortgage payments, do residents pay periodic fees or maintenance charges? If "Yes," describe what these charges cover and how they are determined.	☐ **Yes**	☐ **No**
3a	Is your housing affordable to low income residents? If "Yes," describe how your housing is made affordable to low-income residents. **Note:** Revenue Procedure 96-32, 1996-1 C.B. 717, provides guidelines for providing low-income housing that will be treated as charitable. (At least 75% of the units are occupied by low-income tenants or 40% are occupied by tenants earning not more than 120% of the very low-income levels for the area.)	☐ **Yes**	☐ **No**
b	Do you impose any restrictions to make sure that your housing remains affordable to low-income residents? If "Yes," describe these restrictions.	☐ **Yes**	☐ **No**
4	Do you provide social services to residents? If "Yes," describe these services.	☐ **Yes**	☐ **No**

Form **1023** (Rev. 12-2017)

Schedule G. Successors to Other Organizations

1a Are you a **successor** to a **for-profit organization**? If "Yes," explain the relationship with the ☐ **Yes** ☐ **No**
   predecessor organization that resulted in your creation and complete line 1b.

b Explain why you took over the activities or assets of a for-profit organization or converted from for-profit
   to nonprofit status.

2a Are you a successor to an organization other than a for-profit organization? Answer "Yes" if you have ☐ **Yes** ☐ **No**
   taken or will take over the activities of another organization; or you have taken or will take over 25% or
   more of the fair market value of the net assets of another organization. If "Yes," explain the relationship
   with the other organization that resulted in your creation.

b Provide the tax status of the predecessor organization.

c Did you or did an organization to which you are a successor previously apply for tax exemption under ☐ **Yes** ☐ **No**
   section 501(c)(3) or any other section of the Code? If "Yes," explain how the application was resolved.

d Was your prior tax exemption or the tax exemption of an organization to which you are a successor ☐ **Yes** ☐ **No**
   revoked or suspended? If "Yes," explain. Include a description of the corrections you made to
   re-establish tax exemption.

e Explain why you took over the activities or assets of another organization.

3 Provide the name, last address, and EIN of the predecessor organization and describe its activities.

   Name: _____   **EIN:** _____

   Address: _____

4 List the owners, partners, principal stockholders, officers, and governing board members of the predecessor organization.
   Attach a separate sheet if additional space is needed.

Name	Address	Share/Interest (If a for-profit)

5 Do or will any of the persons listed in line 4, maintain a working relationship with you? If "Yes," describe ☐ **Yes** ☐ **No**
   the relationship in detail and include copies of any agreements with any of these persons or with any
   for-profit organizations in which these persons own more than a 35% interest.

6a Were any assets transferred, whether by gift or sale, from the predecessor organization to you? If "Yes," ☐ **Yes** ☐ **No**
   provide a list of assets, indicate the value of each asset, explain how the value was determined, and
   attach an appraisal, if available. For each asset listed, also explain if the transfer was by gift, sale, or
   combination thereof.

b Were any restrictions placed on the use or sale of the assets? If "Yes," explain the restrictions. ☐ **Yes** ☐ **No**

c Provide a copy of the agreement(s) of sale or transfer.

7 Were any debts or liabilities transferred from the predecessor for-profit organization to you? ☐ **Yes** ☐ **No**
   If "Yes," provide a list of the debts or liabilities that were transferred to you, indicating the amount of
   each, how the amount was determined, and the name of the person to whom the debt or liability is
   owed.

8 Will you lease or rent any property or equipment previously owned or used by the predecessor for-profit ☐ **Yes** ☐ **No**
   organization, or from persons listed in line 4, or from for-profit organizations in which these persons own
   more than a 35% interest? If "Yes," submit a copy of the lease or rental agreement(s). Indicate how the
   lease or rental value of the property or equipment was determined.

9 Will you lease or rent property or equipment to persons listed in line 4, or to for-profit organizations in ☐ **Yes** ☐ **No**
   which these persons own more than a 35% interest? If "Yes," attach a list of the property or equipment,
   provide a copy of the lease or rental agreement(s), and indicate how the lease or rental value of the
   property or equipment was determined.

Form **1023** (Rev. 12-2017)

Schedule H. Organizations Providing Scholarships, Fellowships, Educational Loans, or Other Educational Grants to Individuals and Private Foundations Requesting Advance Approval of Individual Grant Procedures

Section I   *Names of individual recipients are not required to be listed in Schedule H.*

Public charities and private foundations complete lines 1a through 7 of this section. See the instructions to Part X if you are not sure whether you are a public charity or a private foundation.

1a	Describe the types of educational grants you provide to individuals, such as scholarships, fellowships, loans, etc.
b	Describe the purpose and amount of your scholarships, fellowships, and other educational grants and loans that you award.
c	If you award educational loans, explain the terms of the loans (interest rate, length, forgiveness, etc.).
d	Specify how your program is publicized.
e	Provide copies of any solicitation or announcement materials.
f	Provide a sample copy of the application used.

2 Do you maintain case histories showing recipients of your scholarships, fellowships, educational loans, or other educational grants, including names, addresses, purposes of awards, amount of each grant, manner of selection, and relationship (if any) to officers, trustees, or donors of funds to you? If "No," refer to the instructions.   ☐ **Yes**   ☐ **No**

3 Describe the specific criteria you use to determine who is eligible for your program. (For example, eligibility selection criteria could consist of graduating high school students from a particular high school who will attend college, writers of scholarly works about American history, etc.)

4a Describe the specific criteria you use to select recipients. (For example, specific selection criteria could consist of prior academic performance, financial need, etc.)

b Describe how you determine the number of grants that will be made annually.

c Describe how you determine the amount of each of your grants.

d Describe any requirement or condition that you impose on recipients to obtain, maintain, or qualify for renewal of a grant. (For example, specific requirements or conditions could consist of attendance at a four-year college, maintaining a certain grade point average, teaching in public school after graduation from college, etc.)

5 Describe your procedures for supervising the scholarships, fellowships, educational loans, or other educational grants. Describe whether you obtain reports and grade transcripts from recipients, or you pay grants directly to a school under an arrangement whereby the school will apply the grant funds only for enrolled students who are in good standing. Also, describe your procedures for taking action if the terms of the award are violated.

6 Who is on the selection committee for the awards made under your program, including names of current committee members, criteria for committee membership, and the method of replacing committee members?

7 Are relatives of members of the selection committee, or of your officers, directors, or **substantial contributors** eligible for awards made under your program? If "Yes," what measures are taken to ensure unbiased selections?   ☐ **Yes**   ☐ **No**

Note: If you are a private foundation, you are not permitted to provide educational grants to **disqualified persons**. Disqualified persons include your substantial contributors and foundation managers and certain family members of disqualified persons.

Section II   Private foundations complete lines 1a through 4f of this section. Public charities do not complete this section.

1a If we determine that you are a private foundation, do you want this application to be considered as a request for advance approval of grant making procedures?   ☐ **Yes**   ☐ **No**   ☐ **N/A**

b For which section(s) do you wish to be considered?

- 4945(g)(1)—Scholarship or fellowship grant to an individual for study at an educational institution   ☐
- 4945(g)(3)—Other grants, including loans, to an individual for travel, study, or other similar purposes, to enhance a particular skill of the grantee or to produce a specific product   ☐

2 Do you represent that you will (1) arrange to receive and review grantee reports annually and upon completion of the purpose for which the grant was awarded, (2) investigate diversions of funds from their intended purposes, and (3) take all reasonable and appropriate steps to recover diverted funds, ensure other grant funds held by a grantee are used for their intended purposes, and withhold further payments to grantees until you obtain grantees' assurances that future diversions will not occur and that grantees will take extraordinary precautions to prevent future diversions from occurring?   ☐ **Yes**   ☐ **No**

3 Do you represent that you will maintain all records relating to individual grants, including information obtained to evaluate grantees, identify whether a grantee is a disqualified person, establish the amount and purpose of each grant, and establish that you undertook the supervision and investigation of grants described in line 2?   ☐ **Yes**   ☐ **No**

Form **1023** (Rev. 12-2017)

Schedule H. Organizations Providing Scholarships, Fellowships, Educational Loans, or Other Educational Grants to Individuals and Private Foundations Requesting Advance Approval of Individual Grant Procedures *(Continued)*

| **Section II** | Private foundations complete lines 1a through 4f of this section. Public charities do not complete this section. *(Continued)* |

4a Do you or will you award scholarships, fellowships, and educational loans to attend an educational institution based on the status of an individual being an *employee of a particular employer?* If "Yes," complete lines 4b through 4f.   ☐ **Yes**   ☐ **No**

b Will you comply with the seven conditions and either the percentage tests or facts and circumstances test for scholarships, fellowships, and educational loans to attend an educational institution as set forth in Revenue Procedures 76-47, 1976-2 C.B. 670, and 80-39, 1980-2 C.B. 772, which apply to inducement, selection committee, eligibility requirements, objective basis of selection, employment, course of study, and other objectives? (See lines 4c, 4d, and 4e, regarding the percentage tests.)   ☐ **Yes**   ☐No

c Do you or will you provide scholarships, fellowships, or educational loans to attend an educational institution to employees of a particular employer?   ☐ **Yes**   ☐ **No**   ☐ **N/A**

If "Yes," will you award grants to 10% or fewer of the eligible applicants who were actually considered by the selection committee in selecting recipients of grants in that year as provided by Revenue Procedures 76-47 and 80-39?   ☐ **Yes**   ☐ **No**

d Do you provide scholarships, fellowships, or educational loans to attend an educational institution to children of employees of a particular employer?   ☐ **Yes**   ☐ **No**   ☐ **N/A**

If "Yes," will you award grants to 25% or fewer of the eligible applicants who were actually considered by the selection committee in selecting recipients of grants in that year as provided by Revenue Procedures 76-47 and 80-39? If "No," go to line 4e.   ☐ **Yes**   ☐ **No**

e If you provide scholarships, fellowships, or educational loans to attend an educational institution to children of employees of a particular employer, will you award grants to 10% or fewer of the number of employees' children who can be shown to be eligible for grants (whether or not they submitted an application) in that year, as provided by Revenue Procedures 76-47 and 80-39?   ☐ **Yes**   ☐ **No**   ☐ **N/A**

If "Yes," describe how you will determine who can be shown to be eligible for grants without submitting an application, such as by obtaining written statements or other information about the expectations of employees' children to attend an educational institution. If "No," go to line 4f.

Note: Statistical or sampling techniques are not acceptable. See Revenue Procedure 85-51, 1985-2 C.B. 717, for additional information.

f If you provide scholarships, fellowships, or educational loans to attend an educational institution to *children of employees of a particular employer* without regard to either the 25% limitation described in line 4d, or the 10% limitation described in line 4e, will you award grants based on facts and circumstances that demonstrate that the grants will not be considered compensation for past, present, or future services or otherwise provide a significant benefit to the particular employer? If "Yes," describe the facts and circumstances that you believe will demonstrate that the grants are neither compensatory nor a significant benefit to the particular employer. In your explanation, describe why you cannot satisfy either the 25% test described in line 4d or the 10% test described in line 4e.   ☐ **Yes**   ☐ **No**

Form **1023** (Rev. 12-2017)

Form 1023 Checklist

(Revised December 2017)

Application for Recognition of Exemption under Section 501(c)(3) of the Internal Revenue Code

Note: Retain a copy of the completed Form 1023 in your permanent records. Refer to the General Instructions regarding Public Inspection of approved applications.

Check each box to finish your application (Form 1023). Send this completed Checklist with your filled-in application. If you have not answered all the items below, your application may be returned to you as incomplete.

☐ Assemble the application and materials in this order.
- Form 1023 Checklist
- Form 2848, *Power of Attorney and Declaration of Representative* (if filing)
- Form 8821, *Tax Information Authorization* (if filing)
- Expedite request (if requesting)
- Application (Form 1023 and Schedules A through H, as required)
- Articles of organization
- Amendments to articles of organization in chronological order
- Bylaws or other rules of operation and amendments
- Documentation of nondiscriminatory policy for schools, as required by Schedule B
- Form 5768, Election/Revocation of Election by an Eligible Section 501(c)(3) Organization To Make Expenditures To Influence Legislation (if filing)
- All other attachments, including explanations, financial data, and printed materials or publications. Label each page with name and EIN.

☐ User fee payment placed in envelope on top of checklist. DO NOT STAPLE or otherwise attach your check or money order to your application. Instead, just place it in the envelope.

☐ Employer Identification Number (EIN)

☐ Completed Parts I through XI of the application, including any requested information and any required Schedules A through H.
- You must provide specific details about your past, present, and planned activities.
- Generalizations or failure to answer questions in the Form 1023 application will prevent us from recognizing you as tax exempt.
- Describe your purposes and proposed activities in specific easily understood terms.
- Financial information should correspond with proposed activities.

☐ Schedules. Submit only those schedules that apply to you and check either "Yes" or "No" below.

Schedule A	Yes ___	No ___	Schedule E	Yes ___	No ___
Schedule B	Yes ___	No ___	Schedule F	Yes ___	No ___
Schedule C	Yes ___	No ___	Schedule G	Yes ___	No ___
Schedule D	Yes ___	No ___	Schedule H	Yes ___	No ___

☐ An exact copy of your complete articles of organization (creating document). Absence of the proper purpose and dissolution clauses is the number one reason for delays in the issuance of determination letters.
- Location of Purpose Clause from Part III, line 1 (Page, Article and Paragraph Number) _____
- Location of Dissolution Clause from Part III, line 2b or 2c (Page, Article and Paragraph Number) or by operation of state law _____

☐ Signature of an officer, director, trustee, or other official who is authorized to sign the application.
- Signature at Part XI of Form 1023.

☐ Your name on the application must be the same as your legal name as it appears in your articles of organization.

Send completed Form 1023, user fee payment, and all other required information, to:

Internal Revenue Service
Attention: EO Determination Letters
Stop 31
P.O. Box 12192
Covington, KY 41012-0192

If you are using express mail or a delivery service, send Form 1023, user fee payment, and attachments to:

Internal Revenue Service
Attention: EO Determination Letters
Stop 31
201 West Rivercenter Boulevard
Covington, KY 41011